What people are saying about …

THE FRESH EYES SERIES

"I heard Doug speak over a decade ago on the feeding of the five thousand, and I still remember what he said. He brought the familiar story to life in a way that made me see it all unfold. I remember thinking, *What would I have done if I'd been there that day with Jesus?* That's why Doug's writing is so valuable. God recorded these events in His Word and Doug takes readers to those moments in history and makes them relatable and best of all, memorable."

—**Robin Jones Gunn**, bestselling author
of over ninety books including the Christy
Miller series and *Victim of Grace*

"On a visit to Japan, our translator asked an artist working in gold leaf how it felt to be surrounded by such expensive materials. The artist replied, 'I've been working with gold so long, I've forgotten it's value.' I know I've felt that exact way when it comes to reading the Word of God. I've been working/reading/studying it for so long, I'm ashamed to say that sometimes, even though I love God's Word, I've forgotten it's value. That's why I'm so grateful for Fresh Eyes. Doug has taken the familiar stories of Scripture, and given us new ideas to ponder, angles to look from, and context to understand. A reminder of the richness and value that surrounds us every day."

—**Kathi Lipp**, bestselling author of *The Husband Project*, *Clutter Free*, and *Overwhelmed*

"The Fresh Eyes series is nothing less than amazing—the most profound, to the point, original, awe-inspiring, and challenging writings about Jesus and the Bible I have ever read or imagined! I was immediately stunned by how the subject matter is exactly what I've always been looking for in Scripture! I hope there will be millions of Christians like me who learn to see Scripture with fresh eyes."

—**Jorge Casas**, bassist, Grammy-award winning producer

"These books are a hit. Doug has found a profound and compelling way to have the reader (ordinary people like you and me) have the eyes of our hearts enlightened. I have read the entire Bible, front to back, for the past fourteen years. In these books, I have gained new insight into Bible sayings, Jesus' miracles, and Jesus' parables. I gained fresh insight into what God is saying to me. In my 162 MLB game schedule, each day brings new excitement. Doug's writing and dissecting of verses make each verse exciting as I grew deeper in my relationship with our Lord."

—**David Jauss**, Major League baseball coach, Pittsburgh Pirates

"Jesus spoke of unique teachers who were able to bring 'new treasures' out of their storerooms (Matt. 13:52). Doug Newton is an extraordinary author who brings us 'new treasure' in this Fresh Eyes series. This series imparts the rare gift of seeing Scripture with fresh eyes, thus igniting fresh fire in our lives for Jesus and His mission. I highly recommend this series for anyone desiring a personal revival and an expanded faith for how greatly God can use their lives. I experienced this for myself as I read Doug's life-giving words!"

—**Larry Walkemeyer**, D.Min.; pastor; church planter; Director of Equipping—Exponential; author of *15 Characteristics of Effective Pastors*

"Doug Newton is a skilled and passionate communicator as well as a trusted, wise guide both from the pulpit and the printed page. His Fresh Eyes series draws from clear thought, engaged storytelling, and a worthy message to help readers marvel anew over God's love and sustain their faith in the face of today's challenges."

—**Ivan L. Filby**, PhD, president of Greenville University, IL

"For many who cherish the Bible as God's Word, a daily experience with the Bible has no greater impact than a weather report, an Op-Ed piece, or a blog post. This is because few believers actually read the Bible much and, when they do, they give it only superficial attention. In the Fresh Eyes series, Doug Newton demonstrates how familiar miracle stories, well-known parables, and often-cited gospel sayings can come alive with power to expose small and limited horizons and expand them to wider and deeper perceptions of kingdom reality then draw you in as Newton teases out life-changing biblical implications."

—**Bishop David W. Kendall**, PhD, Free Methodist Church—USA

"For decades Doug Newton's clear and crisp teaching has captured the deep and transformative truths of God's Word. What a treasure to have these rich and wonderful insights through Fresh Eyes. You will be deeply touched and truly challenged by this brilliant master teacher. What a gift!"

—**David Goodnight**, JD, LLM,
partner at Stoel Rives, LLP

"Doug Newton reminds us that the compelling teachings and miracles of Jesus were not just clever events to create believers but were the examples of everyday life. In captivating stories, Newton refocuses us to remember that staying 'tuned in' in prayerful communion opens our eyes to the reality that miracles happen all around us all the time."

—**Hal Conklin**, president of USA
Green Communities, former mayor
of Santa Barbara, California

"Fresh Eyes is a crucial series for our hyper-connected world. Doug Newton equips readers with the tools needed to slow down, open our eyes, and unlock the true meaning of the inspired stories of the Bible. As he has done from the pulpit for many years, Doug provides rich guidance and training with easy-to-understand language and stories that make things click. Fresh Eyes is a must-have for anyone who wants to be equipped to wrestle with the meaning of Scripture and the many ways it applies to the hustle and bustle of twenty-first-century living.

—**Hugo Perez**, chief marketing
officer, OHorizons Foundation

DOUG NEWTON

FRESH

EYES

ON

FAMOUS
BIBLE
SAYINGS

Discovering New Insights in Familiar Passages

DAVID C COOK

transforming lives together

FRESH EYES ON FAMOUS BIBLE SAYINGS
Published by David C Cook
4050 Lee Vance Drive
Colorado Springs, CO 80918 U.S.A.

Integrity Music Limited, a Division of David C Cook
Eastbourne, East Sussex BN23 6NT, England

The graphic circle C logo is a registered trademark of David C Cook.

Unless otherwise noted, all Scripture quotations are taken from THE HOLY
BIBLE, NEW INTERNATIONAL VERSION®, NIV® Copyright © 1973, 1978,
1984, 2011 by Biblica, Inc.® Used by permission. All rights reserved worldwide.
Scripture quotations marked ESV are taken from the ESV® Bible (The Holy
Bible, English Standard Version®), copyright © 2001 by Crossway, a publishing
ministry of Good News Publishers. Used by permission. All rights reserved; KJV
are taken from the King James Version of the Bible. (Public Domain.); NASB
are taken from the New American Standard Bible®, copyright © 1960, 1995
by The Lockman Foundation. Used by permission. (www.Lockman.org).
The author has added italics to Scripture quotations for emphasis.

LCCN 2018932041
ISBN 978-1-4347-1213-4
eISBN 978-1-4347-1216-5

© 2018 Douglas M. Newton
Published in association with the literary agency of Books & Such
Literary Management, 52 Mission Circle, Suite 122, PMB 170,
Santa Rosa, CA 95409-5370, www.booksandsuch.com.

The Team: Alice Crider, Mick Silva, Amy Konyndyk,
Rachael Stevenson, Diane Gardner, Susan Murdock
Cover Design: Nick Lee

Printed in the United States of America
First Edition 2018

1 2 3 4 5 6 7 8 9 10

051618

*To my daughters, Kelcey and Erin, who
from day one have respected their earthly
father's words but, more importantly, live
in faithful, loving response to their heavenly
Father's words—and not just the easy ones.*

CONTENTS

ACKNOWLEDGMENTS

The man who was, I think, the most creative and engaging preacher I ever heard died in a car crash when I was in sixth grade. I say "I think" because I never really cared about what he was saying at the time. After all, I was only twelve years old, and there were better things to do to pass the time until noon. But I sensed his impact because of the way my parents and all the other adults in my small country church reacted when he preached. They loved it—and him. The congregation leaned forward. Even our 1965 Chevy Impala seemed eager for church every Sunday!

Carl Johnson, our pastor, a journalism grad student at Syracuse University, apparently mixed humor with ways to enter a biblical text that disposed of the traditional three-point sermon with the tearjerker story at the end. Again I say "apparently" because I didn't get the jokes or insights; I just heard the appreciative laughs and appreciable amens around me.

And even though I vowed at age ten I would never be a preacher, I knew what a preacher needed to be from sitting in the pews Sunday after Sunday inside that atmosphere of rapt attention. So when I did eventually become a pastor-teacher—even though my "call" was initially more coincidental than covenantal—I had an unchosen but unwavering passion: to help people see the Bible with fresh eyes and expectancy.

Now that forty years of preaching and teaching have passed, I can see how the "spirit" of Carl Johnson—I should really capitalize that word—permeated and still permeates how I approach biblical examination and exposition. That Spirit led me to preach two back-to-back sermons one Sunday while running the entire time on a treadmill in order to illustrate the significance of Peter's use of the word *spoudazo* (meaning "make every effort") in 2 Peter 1:5. It led me to build and preach inside a black cloth-covered enclosure just so I could come to the finale and demonstrate with one thrust of a spear how praise and proclamation pierce spiritual darkness.

I never wanted to use gimmicks, but very often the Lord prompted me to see something unusual and use something visual. As a result, I have enjoyed kind comments from the people of four congregations over the years telling me how much they looked forward to what I was going to do and say on Sunday. I always deflected those comments with "You mean, what the *Lord* is going to say." And they would nod, "Of course."

However, the fact remains that the human roles of careful study and creativity combine to make what God wants to say through His Word clear and compelling. Creativity is inherently mnemonic.

At the outset of this Fresh Eyes series, I want to acknowledge Carl Johnson and the gifted thinkers and teachers he represents who have inspired me toward preaching that reveals rather than regurgitates truth. And even more, I thank all the congregations of believers among whom I have lived and served who have shown me what it looks like to lean forward to hear a word from the Lord: for three years with the kids of the South Presbyterian Church high school group in Syracuse, New York; for thirteen years with the people of Fountain Square Church in Bowling Green, Kentucky; for five years with the students and staff of the Oakdale Christian Academy boarding school in Jackson, Kentucky; and for the past eleven years with the people of Greenville (IL) Free Methodist Church.

For fifteen years I served as editor of *Light & Life*, the denominational magazine of the Free Methodist Church. This was also a significant time in my life when I learned to communicate more broadly through writing to people I would never see from the Sunday pulpit. That opportunity and training would never have occurred without the courage of four bishops who hired me—a pastor with no journalism or seminary degree—simply because I had what they regarded as an anointed, albeit "unsafe" (their word), creative approach to communication.

My role as editor led to my speaking periodically at writer's conferences—most often at the renowned Mount Hermon

Christian Writers Conference. I owe a great debt of thanks to Dave Talbott, who hardly knew me when inviting me to preach on Palm Sunday in 1998 in the rustic auditorium beneath the praising redwoods to the crowd filled with professional writers. And he continued to do so for several years, even though I had not yet joined the ranks of published authors.

That is where I was first heard and shaped by these professionals, many of whom became friends. One of them, Wendy Lawton, committed herself to me as my agent long before there was any sign I would ever repay her kindness with even a dime of compensation. I couldn't have been given a more gifted, wise, and dedicated agent than she and the Books & Such Literary Agency.

One day she and Janet Grant, founder of the agency, approached me with a clear vision of how to position me as an author. They said, "You need to just do what you do—open people's eyes to Scripture in fresh ways." Within a few months, I had a contract with David C Cook, thanks to them and Alice Crider, senior acquisitions editor, who championed this multi-book project with an accompanying app.

Suddenly I had a contract, and the initial drafts of three books had to be written from scratch in five months. This was a daunting task made more feasible because over the years I have learned how to write with intense focus as my Greenville church staff graciously accommodated my need to get away several times a year to work on various writing projects.

However, when this massive project came along, I needed something more than intense focus. I would need big blocks of time and a sense of the Lord's permission. A series of God-ordained events gave me that green light and changed my ministry responsibilities dramatically. Two of those events involved divine instruction that came miraculously and separately through Ben Dodson and Sarah Vanderkwaak. I am grateful they risked speaking when they could have remained silent. I am also grateful for dear friends Ivan and Kathie Filby, and my gifted superintendent Ben Tolly, for seeing a future ahead of me I would not have imagined.

Alice Crider was gracious enough to honor my request to select my own editor, Mick Silva. We had met at Mount Hermon and had only two casual conversations, but that was enough for me to have confidence in his spiritual sensitivity and professional skills. This initial confidence proved to be well-founded as our friendship grew and as Mick's expertise sharpened and supported the mission and message of the Fresh Eyes books chapter by chapter and line by line.

I was also pleased to have been brought into the David C Cook family at a time when the company was retooling its focus and functions in fresh ways to fulfill its long-standing mission to resource and disciple the church worldwide. That mission, so evident in the processes and people at David C Cook, convinced my wife and me to come under their banner in this project. I have enjoyed how much I have learned every step of the way through the enthusiastic encouragement of Alice Crider, Toben Heim, and the team of people assigned to guide me through this project to completion and distribution: Rachael Stevenson, Diane Gardner, Kayla Fenstermaker, Nick Lee, Susan Murdock, Megan Stengel, Annette Brickbealer, Nathan Landry, and Austin Davco.

Finally, it probably goes without saying, but it is impossible not to shout from the rooftops how much I owe to my family. My two girls, their amazing husbands, and combined five kids. They have not only given me their love and respect over the years, but they have also let me experience what it means to live knowing your kids are proud of you—and tell you! That lubricates the mechanics of life through the grind of large projects like Fresh Eyes.

Then there's Margie. She's my hero, my model, my friend, my encourager. There has been a sparkle in her eyes from the very beginning of being "us" that comes from her love for Jesus. That sparkle is my north star. It keeps me navigating through life, no matter what comes, toward greater love for the Lord. Without that sparkle in her eyes, my own would have long since grown dim with cares and worries and doubts preventing me from seeing anything—life itself or its Author—with fresh eyes. But when you have someone who loves you unconditionally in such a way that helps you know the love of God, your eyes will sparkle too with expectancy of seeing new and fresh things in the world and in the Word.

Doug Newton

March 2018

ABOUT THE FRESH EYES SERIES

What if the commonplace understanding of a Bible story or a well-known Scripture passage is the very thing keeping us from seeing the text in a new, life-transforming way?

We all find ourselves facing this problem when we study the Bible. We believe Scripture is living and powerful. But many of us, after a genuine encounter with God followed by faithful Bible study and many sermons, became so familiar with Scripture that it lost its impact. The Bible became a book of riddles to be solved. Once we "figured out what a passage meant," we checked it off and moved on. We've seen these stories too many times, and everyone who's been a Christian for even a year or two knows how that voracious appetite for the Word quickly fades.

Pastors and Bible teachers craft a message from a particular text, and the lesson they convey becomes the way we understand the passage from that point on. Within a few short years, it feels like we're hearing the same thing over and over again. We begin to approach the Bible with less zip and zeal. Familiarity may not always breed contempt, but it does tend to breed complacency.

Yet consider Jesus' remedy: "You have heard that it was said, but I tell you …" He invited His listeners to break away from well-worn thinking to see something new and different. We need to look with fresh eyes at what we think we know well. A passage's common interpretation may have taken a wrong turn somewhere along the line and been passed along like an urban legend. The application may need to shift in a different direction or include something not considered before. There's new hope for our lives to change when we can say, "I never saw it that way before."

My primary mission with this book series is not to share new insights I've uncovered. My greater desire is to reveal specific techniques that will allow you to make new discoveries about familiar passages that can revive your love for the infinite Word and transform your work in teaching and testimony.

The interactive section at the end of each chapter includes a "Vision Check," which describes Fresh Eyes study techniques. These reveal how I found something new and inspiring by reexamining the text and context of a passage, the life situations involved, the cultural perspectives reflected, and other details and how I began to see Scripture more imaginatively. You'll also find more resources at dougnewton.com and on the Fresh Eyes app to help you gain additional insights.

I pray you find the treasures in God's Word are truly inexhaustible when you come with fresh eyes.

INTRODUCTION

I once spoke at a Christian college for a week of chapel services and showed a film clip from the classic movie *Rudy*, in which the unlikely hero is an undersized football player for Notre Dame who never got to play until the last seconds of the final game of his senior year, Rudy made the game-ending tackle, and his teammates hoisted him on their shoulders. The students in my audience cheered as the music soared and chanted, "Rudy! Rudy! Rudy!" with the film's stadium crowd. The room pulsed with energy and excitement.

Then I replayed the scene's final moments again. The same cheers, but fewer and less strong. Then I played it again. And again. By the sixth time, no one in that chapel was cheering. A smattering of polite applause, and mostly confused faces, evidenced my audience's waning interest.

What had changed? I showed the same scene. The volume of the cheers in the movie was as loud as before. But the thrill had diminished through repetition. The danger, I explained to the students, is that the weekly rehearsing of the gospel in our churches can become exactly like this.

It's the same with these famous Bible sayings. The more well-known they become, the more they get preached and taught and printed on T-shirts and calendars, the less their message inspires us. The life-changing truths haven't changed; we've just gotten used to them. Of course, no one wants that to happen, but it seems a fact of life that enthusiasm dies with familiarity.

What if that didn't have to happen with the Bible? What if those old famous sayings could be made new? What if we could see them afresh as revelation and inspiration? And what if you could learn to rediscover a passage's original insights and find an endless shelf life in such familiar passages all on your own? That's what this book is about.

Each chapter focuses on one famous Bible saying, which together organize loosely into two categories: teachings on kingdom *morality* and teachings on kingdom *ministry*. We'll reconsider and reframe each saying much as Jesus did with familiar Old Testament passages in the Sermon on the Mount. "You have heard that it was said … but I tell you …" We'll do this not to abolish what came before but to renew it and even take it further. You'll see beyond what you've always heard or already thought and discover some refreshing and challenging ideas. But my greatest hope is to give you the tools to reframe Scripture yourself. New inspiration from our ancient Scriptures could transform our churches and our own lives. We would go into worship services, small groups, and daily conversations with transferable truths and true enthusiasm about the timeless and inexhaustible treasures available in God's Word.

I am excited to welcome you into the pages of this book. I'm convinced when you realize what God has given you to discover in these passages, it becomes impossible to read Scripture and *not* feel like celebrating, raising up our Hero on our shoulders, and shouting, "Jesus! Jesus!"

1

WHAT MAKES THE OLD CROSS SO RUGGED?

Take Up Your Cross

Luke 9:23

If we're supposed to follow Jesus, we'd better
make sure we know what His cross is like.

Do we really think the best way to prove God's love is to splash blood all over the crucifixion story? We essentially do all year long but especially during the Easter season. When preachers want to hammer home the enormity of Jesus' sacrifice, they often resort to giving detailed descriptions of His suffering. They try to do verbally what Mel Gibson did visually in his 2004 blockbuster *The Passion of the Christ*. Who could watch without wincing? Gibson took us inside Jesus' torn flesh deeper than we wanted to go. Sermons can't match cinema.

But we try. Preachers describe the whips that tore Jesus' flesh. They point to where the nails were likely driven in— through the wrists, not the palms—and why: Jesus' body weight would have ripped His hands loose between His middle and ring fingers. Attempting to add visual emphasis to the verbal explanation, they demonstrate with their bodies how being hung in that fashion would have constricted His airways. In order to take a breath, Jesus would have had to push down on the nails driven through His feet. Excruciating.

Some drag out the description to simulate the length of Jesus' suffering, until they finally talk about the spear and the watery blood gushing as the spear's tip penetrated the pericardial sac, adding notes of medical science to make it sound more believable, more factual. All this is designed to attract the listener to God's love through the most repulsive image of death imaginable.

You've likely heard similar descriptions as well. Ironically, such painful portrayals have helped create a severe misunderstanding of the nature of the cross we are supposed to "take up" in order to follow Jesus. To a degree, understanding what a crucifixion really involved—and what Jesus likely endured—may help some listeners both grasp God's love and understand something unfamiliar to our culture. As such, preachers who teach this way do so with commendable motivations. However, a heavy-handed, unbalanced focus on Christ's suffering can lead to some significant, though unintended, misunderstandings.

NOT JUST ANY KIND OF SUFFERING

When preachers belabor the many horrific elements of Jesus' death, it is understandable that people primarily equate the cross with suffering. Consequently, we tend to perceive any unwanted or unfair suffering as our "cross to bear." Whether we encounter a thoughtless person at work or a traumatic experience, we may pray about such things, but most of us still think there's simply nothing to be done about them. It's injustice that God wants us to learn from. Didn't Jesus warn us there'd be trials?

Yet suffering in and of itself, even for godly reasons or with a godly attitude, does not necessarily constitute the cross of Christ. Perhaps you are finding it hard to imagine a Christian even saying this. How can this be?

Simple. Something is missing. The true cross has a specific purpose: accepting the burden of suffering in order to provide a remedy for the suffering of others. Jesus paid the penalty for our sin by taking our place. When Jesus was sentenced to death, He had committed no wrong. He deserved no punishment. We, on the other hand, owed God an unpayable debt because of our many, many sins committed out of negligence, ignorance, disobedience, and rebellion. The death sentence hung justly over our heads. When Jesus hung on the cross, He suffered the consequences of our failures, pure and simple, so we could be forgiven. Our sin wasn't His fault, His problem, or due to His neglect. Yet He paid the price. He exchanged places with us. He provided the remedy at great personal cost. As Paul put it, "God made him who had no sin to be sin for us, so that in him we might become the righteousness of God" (2 Cor. 5:21).

This is the true character of the cross. It can be stated simply: something isn't a cross until you are paying a personal price to provide a remedy for someone else's suffering whether due to sin, foolishness, or misfortune. So when a person crosses the street to help a neighbor through a financial crisis after getting fired from his job or when missionaries cross the ocean, taking their kids away from grandparents and familiar surroundings, to serve an unreached people group, they are following the way of the cross.

Only when we give up something rightfully ours or put ourselves in harm's way or jeopardize our security for another is it like Jesus' cross—and even then, it only faintly reflects what He endured.

The unsettling thought is that Jesus seems to expect us to do this—*daily*! Even if we could, do we honestly have that many opportunities? I believe we do. There are sometimes dramatic ones, but more often, there are simple daily interactions. But they're always divine moments.

THE CROSS MAY SOMETIMES BE DRAMATIC

As a college freshman, I became our college newspaper's assistant editor. I wanted to be the editor in my sophomore year, but underclassmen weren't allowed to hold that position. I appealed for an exception and was granted approval, provided I study under the editor that year—a college senior.

In a bewildering turn of events, he made a bizarre sexual request of me. I refused, and he threatened suicide if I did not grant his request. Frightened but resolute, I refused again.

Later that week, with the editor present, I informed the faculty adviser of my decision to resign, forfeiting my opportunity to be editor. I remember that night vividly. The adviser was frustrated because he had gone to bat for me to get the rules changed. "Why?" he wondered.

But I wouldn't say why. I knew it was a sacrifice. The editor was agnostic, and I knew his reputation would be ruined if I shared. So I remained silent. But the editor jumped in and bitterly "explained" that my change of heart was due to immaturity and other severe character flaws.

The adviser turned to me, bewildered. "How can you just sit there?" he asked. "If someone was saying about me what he's saying about you, I'd hit him in the mouth."

Wanting to be Christlike in that moment, not sure I was doing the right thing—and even though speaking up is often critically important—I believed in this case my silence and sacrifice, even if ultimately unnecessary, would honor Jesus and He could use it somehow. So I entrusted myself to the One who judges justly and renounced my position on the college newspaper staff.

I completed my college career with a cloud over my head, my reputation damaged. But ten years later that editor wrote me a letter apologizing and sharing his newfound faith, attributing it largely to my testimony of silence under false accusation. And although I thought that episode derailed my track toward journalism, twenty years later, with no further journalistic experience, my denomination unexpectedly asked me to be the editor of its national magazine. It was like a resurrection took place, which mirrored what taking up a true cross should ultimately produce, though often no such direct restoration for our sacrifices seems forthcoming.

THE CROSS OCCURS DAILY

I share that dramatic story to offer hope. We don't always know what to do or whether our decisions for Jesus' way will even matter in the end. But we face choices every day to give up something we may never regain (time, money, credit) to provide something others may never deserve (grace, forgiveness, a second chance). That's the cross.

How do you know when you've arrived at one of these daily "take up your cross" moments? Your insides will resonate and moan with a single question: *Why should I have to be the one?* We hear this voice in small ways every day.

No one ever takes a class to learn this line. Kids aren't taught it in kindergarten like the Pledge of Allegiance. Yet there's probably never been a human being who hasn't said those words exactly, word for word, in his or her native language: *Why should I have to be the one?*

Just as a streak of lightning illuminates your home for a split second, your internal sense of justice instantly highlights the unfairness: *I wasn't the one who made the mistake. I'm not the one to blame.* We reasonably fear enabling mistreatment and worse.

I'm always having to make up for what she doesn't do.

I'm the one always bending over backward.

He never says he's sorry. If we ever make up, it's because I initiate it.

She almost always misses her deadline; then I'm left with too little time and look bad.

But there is no way around it. The true cross of Jesus calls you to lose what you may never regain to give what others may never deserve. And perhaps—but only perhaps—others will see the love of God demonstrated through your grace.

These kinds of situations happen every day, particularly ones involving your use of time and resources. The cross is accepting unfairness. It's receiving poor treatment. It's not fighting back.

THE CROSS WILL ALWAYS BE DIVINE

Taking up the true cross can also mean taking on others' pain when they're victims of improper treatment or have made innocent mistakes.

Years ago, my wife took some city kids on a field trip to the country to expose them to the wonders of nature. She led them high and low through the woods, spying plants, tiny flowers, birds, and bugs. They carved names on tree fungus and made hiking sticks. It was a wonderful couple of hours, until she got back to the landowners' home. When she told them where the kids had gone, they gasped. "Oh no, you took them right through undergrowth full of poison ivy!"

My wife felt heartsick. To think that her desire to inspire them to love nature might actually leave them stricken with terrible allergic reactions and a fear of nature! But in that moment, a hope shot through her—an impression of something, maybe the only thing she could do. Pray. And not just any prayer, but a costly one. "Lord," she prayed, "please protect the kids. If any of them got poison ivy, put it all on me so none of them suffers with it."

Wouldn't you know, the next day poison ivy welted her arms and legs—the worst case she ever had—but none of the kids ever broke out. I don't pretend to understand how and why the Lord chooses to work as He does. But I did wonder, *If He could do that, couldn't He have rid poison ivy from them all without my wife breaking out?* Such questions are hard to answer definitively. However, the apostle Paul pointed us in the right direction when he shared that he thirsted to know Jesus to such a degree that everything else in his life amounted to nothing more than garbage in comparison. As he saw it, "knowing Christ" involves experiencing resurrection power. But it also includes the other side of the coin: "I consider everything a loss because of the surpassing worth of knowing Christ Jesus my Lord, for whose sake I have lost all things.... I want to know Christ—yes, to know and the power of his resurrection and *participation in his sufferings*, becoming like him in his death" (Phil. 3:8, 10).

I know no one more Christlike than my wife. I believe Jesus made her that way. He's making all of us that way. When we suffer for others' sake—whether innocent victims or guilty villains—we enter into His suffering and become like Him. Why would Jesus want to short-circuit that?

It doesn't take preachers splashing blood to make the cross a wonder to behold. It just takes people like my wife showing what the cross is like.

20/20 FOCUS

1. When we suffer in the place of another person, we are truly taking up the cross of Christ. But that doesn't mean other times of suffering are pointless. What other reasons may God have for allowing us to suffer?

2. Why do you think we tend to miss the central nature of the cross—taking on someone else's suffering—when it comes to carrying our cross?

3. This chapter mentions a few examples of daily opportunities to take on the consequences of other people's neglect or mistakes. Can you think of a few examples from your own life or the life of someone you know?

Lord, now that I have a sharper focus on the nature of the cross I am supposed to carry, I realize why You mentioned self-denial first. I never will be able to take up a cross like Yours unless You fulfill the purpose of Your cross in me: set me free from selfishness and fill my heart with Your self-sacrificing love. Amen.

VISION CHECK

A secondary element in a Scripture passage or biblical event that has come to dominate our attention can sometimes overshadow a passage's main point as in this case, in which the popular emphasis on the violence done to Jesus has come to overshadow the purpose of His suffering. Always ask yourself, *What is the primary element in this text or event?*

Read the creation account in Genesis 1, noting its chronological structure. For years the question of a six-day creation process has dominated people's attention. Debates rage and so do people over this issue. Is this a secondary or primary issue in the biblical account? What else might deserve to be raised to a primary position of attention and application? If you make that the issue of greatest importance, do you see the creation account in a new way? See my discoveries by going to dougnewton.com or the Fresh Eyes app.

2

WOULD HAVING

Do unto Others

Luke 6:31

There's only one way to keep
the Golden Rule shiny.

If rarity gave the Golden Rule its value, it wouldn't be worth a plug nickel. Rare it is not. Nearly every religion and philosophical system teaches some form of the Golden Rule (aka "the law of reciprocity") about treating others in ways you want to be treated.

Most of those versions state the rule in the negative. "Do *not* treat others in a way you do *not* want to be treated." For example, six hundred years before Christ's birth the Greek scholar Pittacus wrote, "Do not to your neighbor what you would take ill from him."[1] Soon after but about five thousand miles away, Confucius wrote, "Never impose on others what you would not choose for yourself."[2] In the *Udānavarga*, an early Buddhist collection of "utterances" attributed to the Buddha and his disciples, it is written, "Hurt not others with what pains yourself."[3]

It disturbed me when I first discovered the Golden Rule was not an exclusively Christian contribution to the world. I had assumed that without Jesus uttering this ethical standard, no one would have thought of it or aspired to live according to it. Imagine my disappointment when I discovered that even Wicca, the modern pagan religion centered around witchcraft, promotes a form of the Golden Rule in the *Book of Ways*: "Hear ye these words and heed them well, the words of Dea, thy Mother Goddess, 'I command thee thus, O children of the Earth, that that which ye deem harmful unto thyself, the very same shall ye be forbidden from doing unto another.'"[4]

Troubled by these findings—and to preserve my sense of Christianity's moral superiority—I sought to mark out a new territory of exclusivity. I quickly jumped to a conclusion: all the others state the rule negatively. Do *not* do what you do *not* want others to do to you. *Jesus brought a whole new slant on the rule*, I thought. *It's not about what you shouldn't do to others; it's about what you should do. That's harder.*

Imagine my increased disappointment when I discovered other religions also phrase the rule in the positive form. A passage in the *Mahabharata*, an ancient epic of India, portrays the wise minister Vidura advising King Yudhishthira, "One should behave towards all creatures as he should towards himself."[5]

Double rats! I thought Christian ethics was unique. Again, not true. It turns out that in 1993 at the Parliament of the World's Religions, 143 religious leaders from the world's major faiths signed the "Declaration toward a Global Ethic," which declared the Golden Rule to be one of the common principles they all shared. Signatories included leaders of the Baha'i faith, Brahmanism, Buddhism, Christianity,

Hinduism, Islam, Jainism, Judaism, Native American religions, neo-paganism, Sikhism, Taoism, Theosophist beliefs,
Unitarian Universalism, and Zoroastrianism.[6] It turns out we
Christians must share our favorite moral ideals like toys in
the world's sandbox.

But that's not all. Here's a famous moral story I wish we
could claim as exclusively Christian. Renditions of it are found
in Jewish and Asian cultures. This is a Hindu version.

> The Swami was having a conversation with
> Lord Shiva one day and said, "Lord, I would
> like to know what heaven and hell are like."
> Lord Shiva led the Swami to two doors.
>
> He opened one of the doors and the Swami
> looked in. In the middle of the room was a
> large round table. In the middle of the table
> was a large pot of stew, which smelled delicious
> and made the Swami's mouth water.
>
> The people sitting around the table were
> thin and sickly. They appeared to be famished.
> They were holding spoons with very long
> handles that were strapped to their arms and
> each found it possible to reach into the pot of
> stew and take a spoonful. However, the handle
> was longer than their arms, so they could not
> get the spoons back into their mouths.

The Swami shuddered at the sight of their misery and suffering. Lord Shiva said, "You have seen hell."

They went to the next room and opened the door. It was exactly the same as the first one. There was the large round table with the large pot of stew which made the holy man's mouth water. The people were equipped with the same long-handled spoons, but here the people were well nourished and plump, laughing and talking.

The Swami said, "I don't understand."

"It is simple," said Lord Shiva. "It requires but one skill. You see they have learned to feed each other, while the greedy think only of themselves."[7]

What a great parable! It sounds like something Jesus could have used when He taught the Golden Rule. But alas, it came from a Hindu teacher.

Is the Golden Rule tarnished because it is not exclusively Christian? Not at all. In fact, Christian thinkers like C. S. Lewis have pointed out how moral values common to all religions argue for the existence of not only *a* god but *the* God revealed uniquely through the Christian faith. There is no need to claim that an exclusively Christian context forged the

Golden Rule. The teaching's true luster comes not by its pedigree but by its specificity. For when we look closer, we find it raises an ethical standard that can be reached only through the divine resources of the Christian faith. Look at Jesus' use of *would have*. "Do to others as you *would have* them do to you."

WOULD HAVING VERSUS WANTING

We could simply restate the Golden Rule: do to others what you want them to do to you. Yet many modern Bible translations have resisted that rendition. Why? Probably because *would have* better captures a mental process. When a person writes a Christmas list of their wants and puts those items on a wish list or emails the list to family members, the mental work of wanting is over and done with. That list expresses the person's wants, but once it is posted online, that person may not give it another thought.

In contrast, the mental process involved when you *would have* something draws our attention to the emotional event of desiring. So *would having* is the still-in-process, ongoing act of forming a mental image of what you want. It is that moment when your desire and the object of that desire are both present to your consciousness.

Think of it this way. I like lots of different kinds of food. When I'm hungry, any number of options would satisfy my *want* of nourishment. Hamburger. Pizza. Thai fried rice. Fried chicken. Cannelloni. Roast beef sandwich. Fish and chips. The list can go on and on, which explains my lifelong struggle with my weight. But when I am running errands with my wife and we plan to eat out and she asks, "What do you feel like tonight?" I might need ten to fifteen minutes to come up with an answer. I consider many options. My mind travels from restaurant to restaurant, considering their menus. That's *would having*. And that's when we play the Where Do We Eat? game.

I say, "I chose last time. It's your turn."

Then she says, "No, I chose last time, remember? We did Italian."

Then I say, still trying to pawn off the decision on her, "You only chose Italian because I narrowed it down to two options."

So she says, "Okay. I'll narrow it down to three options."

But even with three options, I can't decide what I *would have*. So I finally play my trump card. "I've been making decisions all day. I really don't want to make another." My wife is such a gracious person, that one usually wins.

The game reveals the difference between *wanting* and *would having*. When you are *would having*, you are actively wrestling with options. You are very conscious of a decision to be made. *Would having* is immediate. Ongoing. Unresolved.

THE MOMENT THE GOLDEN RULE TURNS GOLD

With this in mind, let's turn our attention back to the Golden Rule and the salient question: When do you *would have* when it comes to how someone should treat you? When does your mind get caught up in the conscious act of wishing—of imagining—how a person should act toward you? (You may want to read the following slowly and out loud. Just a suggestion …)

Do you *would have* when a person is already doing what you *would have* them do to you? Of course not. You spend time *would having* only when someone is not doing what you *would have* them do to you and you are imagining what you wish they were doing.

Right here is when the Golden Rule becomes pure gold. At the very time people are *not* doing for you what you *would have* them do for you, that's when you are supposed to do that kind and caring thing for them.

When you aren't getting the thoughtfulness you *would have* them show you—and their disappointing neglect preoccupies your mind—that's precisely the time you are supposed to be thoughtful to them. When people are not treating you with the respect you deserve, that's precisely when you are supposed to treat them with respect.

The gold in the Golden Rule is found precisely in the timing. It's one thing to do nice things for other people who have done them for you. You can do those things anytime—send them a thank-you note for their hard work or offer to help them with a project. But what if they never do those things for you? What if they never show gratitude for all your hard work? What if they never offer to help you when you could use an extra hand? You see, it's a completely different matter to do those very things for them (i.e., what you would have them do for you) right when they are failing to do them for you! That's when the Golden Rule glistens.

THE DIFFERENCE JESUS INTENDS

The Golden Rule found in other religions does promote doing things you would like done for you. However, none of their versions emphasizes the timing we've just identified: giving grace precisely when another does not deserve it. This is the unique slant Jesus intended when He stated the Golden Rule in Luke 6. Let's examine this passage in more detail.

Notice how in each case Jesus expects you to extend grace toward those who are actively engaged in graceless behavior toward you. Your enemies—they are being hateful toward you and cursing you. You *would have* them love you, do good to you, and pray for you instead. But they are not. So Jesus said

to do that for them: "But to you who are listening I say: Love
your enemies, do good to those who hate you, bless those who
curse you, pray for those who mistreat you" (vv. 27–28).

People are striking you and taking from you. You *would
have* them stop hurting and taking and start loving and giving
instead. But they are not doing that. So Jesus said do that for
them: "If someone slaps you on one cheek, turn to them the
other also. If someone takes your coat, do not withhold your
shirt from them. Give to everyone who asks you, and if anyone
takes what belongs to you, do not demand it back. Do to others
as you would have them do to you" (vv. 29–31).

It's easy to be kind to others when they are being kind to
you. There's no particular moral luster to that, Jesus said. "If you
love those who love you, what credit is that to you? Even sinners
love those who love them. And if you do good to those who are
good to you, what credit is that to you? Even sinners do that.
And if you lend to those from whom you expect repayment,
what credit is that to you? Even sinners lend to sinners, expecting to be repaid in full" (vv. 32–34).

But helping your enemies in their time of need? Could
there be anything more golden and godly than that? "But love
your enemies, do good to them, and lend to them without
expecting to get anything back. Then your reward will be great,
and you will be children of the Most High, because he is kind
to the ungrateful and wicked. Be merciful, just as your Father is
merciful" (vv. 35–36).

Do you see the point Jesus repeated and what makes His use of the Golden Rule so different. The brilliance of God's mercy is the gold standard. Jesus' version of the Golden Rule focuses our attention on doing kind and loving things for others precisely when our hearts ache and our lives suffer from others' negligence or nastiness.

For months King Saul sought to destroy David, his divinely appointed replacement. Saul threw spears at David, ran him out of town, and hunted him down. Saul would have mounted David's head on a spike if he could have found him. Then one day the king wandered into a cave for a pit stop (1 Sam. 24). He did not know David was hiding in that cave, which provided David with the perfect opportunity to sneak up on Saul during his moment of preoccupation and put an end to his persecutor. However, because David *would have* Saul show mercy and spare his life, he did that very thing for Saul.

There are many reasons God called David "a man after his own heart" (13:14). Chief among them was how David's mercy mirrored God's. "But God demonstrates his own love for us in this: While we were still sinners, Christ died for us.… For if, while we were God's enemies, we were reconciled to him through the death of his Son, how much more, having been reconciled, shall we be saved through his life!" (Rom. 5:8, 10).

Chick-fil-A's infamous stand opposing gay marriage in 2012 resulted in backlash and boycotts by gay marriage activists. Their efforts marginalized the company and maligned its senior leaders. In spite of the vitriol, Dan Cathy, the company's chief operating officer, slipped behind the headlines to befriend Campus Pride director, Shane Windmeyer, an openly gay man and activist. That act, proven sincere over time, won Windmeyer's respect. Windmeyer said, "Dan expressed a sincere interest in my life, wanting to get to know me on a personal level. He wanted to know about where I grew up, my faith, my family, even my husband, Tommy…. He had to face the issue of respecting my viewpoints and life while not being able to reconcile them with his belief system. He expanded his world without abandoning it. I did as well."[8]

Eventually Windmeyer publicly came out … as Cathy's friend.

There is nothing easier, especially in today's moral climate, than to repay evil for evil. Or at least to pine over what we would have people do for us when they neglect or mistreat us. And there's nothing harder than blessing and loving others in precisely those times. But that's when the Golden Rule shines. That's when you stand at the brink of a choice that can be truly and singularly Christian. That's what Jesus' love makes possible. And beyond question, that's what Jesus would have.

20/20 FOCUS

1. This chapter reveals that some of Christianity's core values, like the Golden Rule, are found

in other religions and even are shared by the secular world. Make a list of two to three other highly touted Christian values that even non-Christians prize and try to practice.

2. What are some other biblical examples of people treating others with grace precisely when they were being mistreated?

3. Can you think of a time someone treated you according to the Golden Rule when you were treating them poorly?

4. Many times we face a moment when someone's neglect or thoughtless behavior disappoints us and we forget to practice the Golden Rule. What could you do to help yourself remember?

Lord, I can see why the Golden Rule is pure gold, but I'm afraid I am not. I get so frustrated and disappointed when people aren't thankful or understanding when I need them to be. Then if they actually have done something unkind, I fume and stew about it. That's exactly when I need Your Holy Spirit to convict me and give me the will to choose gold rather than grudge. Amen.

VISION CHECK

This chapter's Fresh Eyes insights come from appreciating the nuances of the phrase *would have*. Whenever you identify a keyword in a Scripture verse, it's often helpful to ask yourself, *What unique connotation does this word have in comparison with another word the author or character might have used?*

Psalm 139 includes the profoundly humble prayer that begins, "Search me, God …" (v. 23). The psalmist goes on to ask the Lord to see whether there is any "offensive" way in him (v. 24). That's the word the NIV chose when translating a Hebrew word that other versions chose to translate as *wicked* (KJV), *grievous* (ESV), or *hurtful* (NASB). What comes to your mind when you think of the word *offensive* in comparison with these other words? Check out my thoughts on dougnewton.com or the Fresh Eyes app.

3

STOP TRYING TO BE LIKE JESUS

Fruit of the Spirit

Galatians 5:22–23

When you try to be something you're not,
it never turns out the way you hope.

Have you ever watched a guy speed off on a motorcycle with his helmet on backward? I know three high-school girls who did. They were walking down Main Street in Chittenango, New York, chatting away about their day at school. Nearby, a guy with long hair came out of the corner drugstore. They didn't pay much attention, but one noticed he carried a motorcycle helmet under his arm and that he was taking his time mounting his 250cc enduro-type bike. One girl bumped shoulders with another girl, giggled, and looked down at the sidewalk—signals that said it all. "Cute guy. Play it cool …"

Meanwhile, the young denim-clad biker dude had noticed them and started his bike. He revved it several times to grab more attention, and when they looked up, he put on his gloves one finger at a time.

As the girls strolled closer, he tossed his long hair, clearly reveling in the none-too-subtle attention, as if to say, "Watch this!"

And they did. They saw everything, even as he drew out each overconfident movement, revving the engine one last time and then plunking the helmet onto his head … backward, the face mask rubbing his neck and chin straps dangling as he slinked away from the curb. The girls pointed in unified peals of laughter.

Sadly, I know all this because I was the boy. I learned a huge lesson that day when I could do nothing but ride off with my backward helmet and deflated ego: there's nothing worse than trying to be something you're not. And trying to impress others is not just a problem among teenage boys.

Nothing is more pathetic than a seventy-year-old man trying to look and act like a college student. Nothing is more comical than a person without rhythm thinking she can dance. There's nothing more pointless than a high school athlete trying to shoot like LeBron James. And even though it may seem to contradict Scripture, nothing is more futile than a Christian, no matter how devout, trying to be like Jesus. Don't get me wrong. I believe it is possible to be like Jesus, and we should *want* to be. But we won't get there by *trying* to be like Jesus. Before you start boiling the tar and sending out for feathers, grant me a few pages to explain.

The quick reason is this: He's way out of our league. So stop trying.

The only way we can come close to Christlikeness is to experience the enabling and transforming power of God's Spirit. But you don't get the Spirit's aid by sitting back and waiting either. It requires effort. Numerous passages make that point, including Philippians 2:12–13: "*Continue to work out* your salvation with fear and trembling, *for it is God who works in you* to will and to act in order to fulfill his good purpose."

These verses reveal the symbiotic relationship between our efforts and God's internal work of empowerment and transformation. Christlikeness requires much effort on our part, but it is not the effort of "trying to be like Jesus." What kind of effort is it? To answer that question, we turn to the famous list of the fruit of the Spirit in Galatians 5:22–23.

WHAT'S MISSING?

Look at that list. It is interesting and important to notice how many crucial moral traits this list lacks. The missing traits give us clues into the kind of effort required of us. For example, courage is missing. How can anyone progress in Christian development without obedience, and how can anyone obey without courage? Yet courage is not mentioned among the Spirit's fruit.

Think about honesty. None of us can take the first step of repentance without honesty. And without repentance you get nowhere. But nowhere does the Bible say God makes us honest. The same is true of thankfulness and gratitude. Did you realize the lack of thankfulness is a primary cause of God's wrath on all people? "The wrath of God is being revealed from heaven against all the godlessness and wickedness of people, who suppress the truth by their wickedness.… For although they knew God, they neither glorified him as God nor gave thanks to him, but their thinking became futile and their foolish hearts were darkened" (Rom. 1:18, 21).

Thankfulness is just that crucial, and it's required of all people, yet it is not mentioned as specifically supplied by the Spirit.

The list can go on. Diligence. Perseverance. Respect. These are all desperately important moral traits missing from the list of the fruit of the Spirit. Plus, you will find no place in Scripture that promises God's Spirit produces them in us. Very interesting. Yes, circumstances and hardships can stimulate the growth of these traits, and God can orchestrate character-producing circumstances, but does God's Spirit alone produce them? Or are they developed only in concert with God's Spirit, through the exercise of the human will, and in the faith required to experience the Spirit's transforming work?

So you see, Christlikeness is a joint effort between God and us. And why does this matter?

SAY IT WITH ME: SPOOO-DAHH-DZOH!

In 2 Peter 1:3–8, the apostle Peter described how this joint effort enables us to "participate in the divine nature" (v. 4). Peter first affirmed God's role: "His divine power has given us everything we need for a godly life …" (v. 3). But then he spent four verses measuring out the high degree of human effort necessary to become fruit-bearing Christians. Apparently, God wants our cooperation.

The Greek word translated *effort* implies making haste and being zealous to accomplish something. It's based on the memorable-sounding word *spoudazo*. For a fun memory aid, try saying it like an Italian chef tasting his special marinara, "Spooo-dahh-dzoh!"

For Christians to avoid being "ineffective and unproductive" (v. 8), Peter urged his readers to "make every spoudazo." "For this very reason, *make every effort* to add to your faith goodness; and to goodness, knowledge; and to knowledge, self-control; and to self-control, perseverance; and to perseverance, godliness; and to godliness, mutual affection; and to mutual affection, love" (vv. 5–7). God's enabling power to be like Jesus is available. But whether we experience it is largely a matter of spoudazo—making every effort.

Peter tossed the ball into our court with the implied repetition of the word *add*. God does not take full responsibility to "add" goodness, knowledge, and self-control to our faith. We must make the effort, with all spoudazo. But we do not focus our effort on trying to be like Jesus. We direct it toward doing our best with the moral strength and spiritual blessings we've already been given.

Think of the woman who had bled for twelve years (Mark 5:25–34). She had gone to every doctor available and spent all her money on possible cures. Nothing had worked. Then one day she heard Jesus was in the vicinity, so she sought Him out. But the crowd was too dense. She could not get to Him.

She thought, *I don't even need to get His attention. If I can squeeze through the crowd and inch my way close enough to touch the hem of His clothes, I will be healed.* So that's what she did. Risking humiliation and even severe rebuke for being so bold as to intrude, she pressed through, touched Jesus' garment, and experienced healing.

As the story recounts, Jesus sensed power going out from Him without His triggering it, and He stopped dead in His tracks, knowing that someone had just been healed. "Who touched me?" He asked (v. 31). The disciples thought He was crazy to ask since the whole crowd was jostling Him. But Jesus insisted on finding that one particular person. When the lady made herself known, Jesus made His point: she had been healed because of *her* faith (see v. 34).

What gets lost in this story is that her faith was expressed through her effort, her spoudazo. Yes, faith healed her. But she possessed it *and* used it. Without personal exertion, without doing everything she could in her own power, she never would have connected with Jesus for that miracle. In fact, a willingness to exert herself characterized her life before that moment. That's what she had been doing for twelve years: weathering frustration and disappointment but still going to doctor after doctor, believing and using up all her money. That's spoudazo.

Do the moral traits missing from Galatians 5:22–23 reveal our part in the process of becoming more and more like Jesus?

THE SPOUDAZO PARADOX

How does this work? Pick out any godly quality you can think of. Should you give it your best and just keep trying harder to be like Jesus?

Let's say you want to be as patient as Jesus would be with some troublesome person. Pretty sure you can't do that on your own. But maybe what love you already have in your heart can be mustered to produce a certain amount of patience on your own. Or maybe *mustered* isn't the right word. Maybe it's *spoudazo*. If you honestly want the patience of Christ, use all the patience you already have. Don't worry about being as patient as Jesus. Do you see the difference? Focus on what you are capable of, not what you aren't and never will be on your own. And just do that much.

As a road cyclist, I have a goal of someday completing a nine-mile time trial at twenty-three miles per hour—an achievable goal for a sixty-four-year-old. Younger guys in my area are doing it at twenty-nine miles per hour. Should I train for that pace? I doubt I'd ever make it. I'd probably break down my body. So instead, I push myself toward *my* limit, not *theirs*.

Same thing here. You want to be like Jesus, but don't try to be *as good* as Jesus. It's when you push yourself to *your* limit that the miracle happens and God supplies what you lack.

Jesus taught this principle of honest effort and reward. It's illustrated in the parable of the talents (Matt. 25:14–30). A master gave three people varying amounts of money to put to good use for his benefit. Two of the three did just that and generated a return on the money. One of the three did nothing except protect his money from loss. When the master returned to settle their accounts, he rewarded those who had used what they had been given and punished the one who had done nothing. The servants who invested all the master gave them, though entrusted with different amounts, received exactly the same reward. If you are faithful with what you have—however little—more will be given.

Apply this principle to anything our Master gives. Because God created us with willpower, each of us possesses some capacity to act with Christlike qualities. Therefore, if you try to be as patient as *you* can be with what patience He's given, you'll gain a supplemental dose as you do.

Isn't this absolutely freeing? You don't have to be like Jesus by your own willful determination; just be like you—as good as you can be—and you'll become more like Him by the blessing of God!

That's the idea of spoudazo. God's divine power for godliness is available but only to those who are "making every effort" to act on what He's already given, and He'll add to whatever measure of character they already have.

Which now raises two questions.

HONEST ANSWERS NEEDED

Do you know how to spoudazo? Our culture prizes comfort and ease. It tends to shape people who don't like to push themselves to the limits of their own capabilities. So the first question spoudazo challenges us to ask is this: Is there an area of your life where you're working with all your might (i.e., spoudazo-ing) to do the best you can?

I have twin nephews. They didn't like to do much around the house when they were young boys. Their granddad thought they were kind of lazy. However, by the time they were in junior high, they had acquired their black belts in karate and performed well in national competitions. When they went to college, they were excellent hockey players at an NCAA Division I school. As upperclassmen, they began playing guitar and writing their own music, eventually forming a Christian heavy-metal band that went on the road, got a recording contract, and had an album on the shelves in a national big-box store. After college, they entered graduate schools and obtained doctorates in philosophy.

One thing after another, they devoted themselves to their goals with steady exertion—spoudazo. Karate. Hockey. Music. PhDs. And by the way, they both were born with cystic fibrosis, a frightening disease that leaves people who were born with it in the 1980s with a life expectancy of about thirty to thirty-five years. They could have grown up sitting on the couch, fearing too much physical exertion. But they pushed themselves to the edge of their capabilities! Is there any area in your life where you are spoudazo-ing?

The second question is more personal: Are you willing to spoudazo to become like Christ? If so, push yourself to do what you are already capable of doing. Want to have Christlike kindness in the face of ill-treatment or neglect? Be as kind as your heart already knows how to be. *But that gets tiring*, you protest. That's true. It takes tremendous effort to use the right tone of voice when you're frustrated. It's so much easier to snap at someone and be done with it. It takes a huge effort to allow no unwholesome talk but only edifying words to come out of your mouth when someone is acting poorly (Eph. 4:29). It's significantly easier to make that sarcastic comment.

Every day while we contemplate passing on a little criticism or paying someone back with a cold shoulder, our consciences say, "You know better than that. Your heart can do better than that." But it's so much easier not to press our hearts toward forgiveness, understanding, and grace. We can go through our lives saying that we want to be like Christ but demanding too little of our own hearts, even as we expect Him to give us His.

God's "divine power has given us everything we need for a godly life" (2 Pet. 1:3). But we must be willing to do more than wait for the fruit of the Spirit to miraculously appear. We already have the capability of some self-control in the face of abuse, some kindness in the face of criticism, some gentleness in the face of disrespect, and some faithfulness in the face of neglect.

So make every effort—spoudazo—to be as good as you already can be. Push your heart to the level of its capability and you'll be filled with the capabilities of God's heart.

20/20 FOCUS

1. Try to put into your own words the relationship between God's transforming works of grace and your effort.

2. Can a person become honest, grateful, and respectful without becoming a Christian? If so, how do these virtues develop?

3. Name something you have done or are doing that required or still requires spoudazo.

4. Ask the Lord to help you identify some Christlike trait you lack toward which you could put more of your own effort.

Lord, on the one hand, I find a great deal of freedom knowing I don't have to try to measure up to Your impossible standards of character. On the other hand, when I am lacking in areas like

*patience, gentleness, peace, joy, and the other fruit
of the Spirit, I know I can't just sit back and wait
for You to make them happen. Strengthen my
resolve to give my best efforts toward expressing
those virtues and then add to my efforts the blessing of Your Spirit's increase. Amen.*

VISION CHECK

In this chapter we learned how to discover new insights in a familiar
passage by paying attention to what is missing. Do that when you
come across lists (as in the "fruit of the Spirit") or with observations
you make over a span of several chapters in Scripture or between
books of the Bible. For example, why didn't Matthew, Mark, and
Luke include most of the miracles John included in his gospel?
Why does the entire book of Esther never use the word *God*?

Read the New Testament's two versions of the Lord's Prayer
as recorded in Matthew 6:9–13 and Luke 11:2–4. Compare
them with each other as well as with the common version we
often recite in church. What's missing in Luke compared with
Matthew? What's missing in both compared with what we com-
monly recite? Ask the Lord for help as you seek new insights
based on those observations. Check out dougnewton.com or the
Fresh Eyes app to see what I observed.

4

THE IMPORTANCE OF WELL-BUILT SEPTIC TANKS

Neighbors

Luke 10:29

You have neighbors right next door you'll
never meet but you're supposed to love.

"He can't help it. He wasn't brought up to know any better." That was my dad's mantra whenever I pointed out some kid cutting across the neighbor's yard or tracking dirt into the church foyer. Looking back, I'm grateful for his gracious perspective, but at the time it frustrated me. Occasionally I returned a wry imitation of his words when he noted some flaw in my performance: "I can't help it. I wasn't brought up to know any better."

However, his quotable words made a lasting impression on me, and I try to practice the policy of grace he taught. But there's at least one irresponsible act I can never pass off no matter how hard I try: littering.

I enjoy road cycling, so I cover several thousand miles of country roads every year. Hardly a day goes by when I don't see a flattened fast-food bag with its entrails smearing the asphalt or empty cans of beer, soda, and chewing tobacco speckling the roadside. My dad's words always come back to me, but I argue against his grace. *I don't care how they were brought up. This is not a case of family culture. This is a case of a faulty conscience.* Some person rolled down his car window, reached for a crumpled fast-food bag on his front seat, then must have ignored that twinge of conscience just before he thought, *I don't care. I don't want this in my car.* And out it went. The trash-throwers know they shouldn't litter—and not just because the law says so. It's a matter of common decency. You don't just shove something out the window and expect somebody else to deal with your mess. They know better.

One day, however, God's Word rebuked my judgmental spirit as I meditated on the idea of loving my neighbor. I saw how I could be just as thoughtless. Maybe I wasn't chucking cheeseburger wrappers out my car window, but in less-blatant ways I was prone to do something similar. This became clearer as I thought more carefully about the question, "Who is my neighbor?" (Luke 10:29).

OUT OF SIGHT, OUT OF MIND

For five years, I was president of a small Christian boarding school in Appalachia. Throughout its history, it struggled to make ends meet, and the staff always had to be creative to feed the students and care for the facilities with very little money. On one occasion, I had the distinct (with the emphasis on "stinked") privilege of dealing with raw sewage seeping through the basement walls of one of the campus buildings, an old parsonage. As we dug into the situation, we found the smelly explanation.

In the mid-1930s a group of men building the parsonage began laying a cinder block septic tank for the house. Being committed, as many building committees are, to the long-lost eleventh commandment, "Thou shalt save money whereverest thou canst," these resourceful men took their shot at making the *Guinness Book of World Records* under "Ways to Cut Corners to Save Money." They used a foundation wall of the house as one of the septic tank's four walls! If that doesn't immediately strike you as problematic, think about it for a minute.

Is that sinking in?

In fact, it did sink in, and the eroding foundation wall could no longer keep the seepage out. So in 1994, we, the beneficiaries of the aforementioned cost-saving decision, followed the sludge upstream and discovered the not-so-well-hidden source from whence it flowed. Eventually, the problem was solved with a backhoe, a new septic tank (planted well away from the house), and a good stiff northerly wind. And as a bonus of the process, I learned something about loving your neighbor as yourself.

We tend to think of neighbors in geographic terms—someone who lives beside you or nearby. We'd never think of dumping sewage in a neighbor's basement. Yet that's effectively what the corner-cutters did. Their past act piped waste into our present day. We may never bump into them, but they're just as close to us in time as our next-door neighbor is to us in location. The things we do today will directly affect those who immediately follow us. When we leave our table a cluttered mess at the mall food court, we have inconvenienced the family who will sit there after we walk away.

We don't do a very good job thinking about those *chronological neighbors*. We wouldn't dream of taking our trays of wrappers and scraps, dumping them on the table of the people eating lunch beside us, and saying, "We don't feel like dealing with this. You take care of it." Yet that is just what we do to our neighbors in time whenever we leave a mess for other people to clean up or a problem for other people to solve. How is that loving your neighbor?

You must try to see those neighbors in your mind's eye, the ones twenty minutes or twenty years from now. They're relying on you. So consider these general rules of neighborly conduct toward those chronological neighbors.

DON'T SCRIMP

We all like to save money and time, especially when we have less than we need. The pressure to get something done that "fits our budget" and "works for now" tempts us to use duct tape when better-quality work and materials are called for. It is simply not loving your chronological neighbor when you think, *This will last as long as I need it. It'll have to do.*

So for example, if doing a repair job properly on the back deck calls for using pressure-treated lumber, then loving your neighbor means using pressure-treated lumber if you can afford it. *But I don't want to spend that much, and anyway we'll probably sell the house in a couple of years.* Sorry, but that attitude violates Jesus' law of neighbor love. It sounds very much like an Old Testament time when people were tempted not to make helpful loans to needy neighbors because the year for canceling debts was near. God gave a strong warning against this attitude and actually called it a "wicked thought." "Rather be openhanded and freely lend them whatever they need. Be careful not to harbor this wicked thought: 'The seventh year, the year for canceling debts, is near,' so that you do not show ill will toward the needy among your fellow Israelites and give them nothing" (Deut. 15:8–9).

If it irks you to think you have to spend more money than you need to get by for now, think of it as an act of worship of the Lord in two ways. First, imitating the Lord who does all things with excellence is the highest form of worship, higher than the most emotion-filled worship music:

- "Let your light shine before others, that they may see your good deeds and glorify your Father in heaven.... Be perfect, therefore, as your heavenly Father is perfect" (Matt. 5:16, 48).

- "People were overwhelmed with amaze-
  ment. 'He has done everything well,' they
  said" (Mark 7:37).

- "Follow God's example, therefore, as dearly
  loved children and walk in the way of love"
  (Eph. 5:1–2).

Second, helping ensure people's future well-being at your
own expense is an act of self-sacrifice that honors and pleases
the Lord. God designed the year for canceling debts to safe-
guard people's future even if it meant creating an expense for
someone in the present. Those who share the Lord's interest
in caring for people's future enjoy His blessing. Scripture says,
"Give generously to them [by loaning money you will not get
back] and do so without a grudging heart; then because of
this the LORD your God will bless you in all your work and in
everything you put your hand to" (Deut. 15:10).

Because care for people's future aligns with the heart of
God, you can count on His help. Some of us may be living
on "daily bread," striving to be good stewards of what little we
have. God understands. We are simply called to prayerfully
do our best with whatever He has provided us and not give
Him less than that. When we do, we might be surprised at
the sometimes creative—even miraculous—means God uses
to multiply those efforts.

DON'T DIP

This neighbor rule follows logically from the concern for other people's future. There are many ways in which our actions today may undermine the security and well-being of future generations. It doesn't matter how desperate the present might be, if we reach into the next generations' resources in order to make things work out for us today, that is no different from reaching across the fence and taking your next-door neighbor's possessions. No matter what you believe about issues like global warming or the mounting national debt in America, the motive behind taking action now—regardless of what you feel that action should or should not be—comes from a moral conviction to care for the next generations.

However, the issues don't have to be that grandiose. For example, if you are blessed to live into old age, failing health and decreased energy are inevitable. Sooner than later you will want to go through all your belongings in your attic, basement, garage, and closets. If you don't do that before it's too late, someone else will have to spend days and weeks sorting through dusty contents in hundreds of boxes. By leaving it to others, you are choosing to confiscate time that rightfully belongs to their tomorrows. Unless you have asked them whether they are willing to use their time and money to deal with your life leftovers, you are dipping into their possessions without permission. Though the incapacities of old age can sneak up on people, try to plan ahead as much as possible. This is just one example of how our present decisions can rob the next generation—or even the next person coming along.

Conversely, we can also bless our chronological neighbors with kindness that will make their lives easier and their work go quicker. Think of how you clear the table after a big family meal. What do you do? You collect all the plates and silverware and take them to the kitchen counter. Then you scrape off the plates into the trash can and stack them before eventually washing them or putting them in the dishwasher. My wife does that in restaurants. When we finish eating, she consolidates everything into a nice stack easy for the busboy to clear. She also consolidates the trash and used towels and gives the room a once-over before we check out of hotel rooms.

I used to think she was silly. "Why are you doing that? That's someone else's job."

She just smiles—"I know"—and continues undeterred. She's loving the busboys and housekeepers—chronological neighbors I rarely think about. Thanks to her, I've made progress over the years. One day it may come as naturally to me as it does to her.

DO PROTECT

This spirit of loving your chronological neighbors will also keep you alert to potential problems in other people's paths. Even seemingly simple or small things. In fact, our moral development may often advance most by finally seeing and seizing the seemingly trivial opportunities to "do what's right." Sensitizing and fine-tuning the conscience create the alertness and clarity necessary to practice the bigger things.

If you're riding your bike and notice a nail in the road, don't just ride around it—stop and pick it up so it won't puncture some other person's tire, even though that person will never know you spared his or her tire. Or rather than avoiding the gum in the parking lot, pick it up with a scrap of paper so other people won't track it into their houses or have to spend ten minutes trying to scrape it off their soles. You could be preventing a much bigger frustration for the next person. Why not take the time to replace the toilet paper on the roll? Or make the bed? Or leave a kind note? Or express gratitude for that small thing someone did?

These little things don't seem to have eternal significance. They won't directly communicate the gospel or lead a person to faith. They don't require divine wisdom or supernatural power. Even other religions and secular ethics propose similar care and kindness for strangers who come after us. The act itself is not the point of loving your neighbor, whether geographical or chronological. The point is why we do it: to honor the Lord by obeying His command to love our neighbor.

That's our heavenly Father's mantra.

20/20 FOCUS

1. Was this thought of chronological neighbors new to you? Did it make you think of any problem or inconvenience you're dealing with now because others weren't thorough or careful in their work?

2. Are there any decisions you are making or have recently made that will affect others in the future? How might it affect them?

3. This idea of loving chronological neighbors is not beyond us. It's how parents and grandparents think all the time: How will my words and work affect my children ten years from now? We simply need to apply this parental instinct to all our words and work. Think of simple ways you could practice broadening that instinct to include nonfamily chronological neighbors. (For example, think of people who will use the sidewalk in front of your house on a snowy day and shovel beyond the boundaries of your own property. Think of the workers who will be collecting your curbside trash and pile it in ways that will be easier for them to pick up.)

Lord, everything good happening in my life is something You planned long before I was born. I can't think that far in advance, but certainly I can look further down the road than I normally do. Help me be more conscious of the people who are coming along in the future. Prompt me to think loving thoughts and take helpful actions for them, even those I will never know. Amen.

VISION CHECK

Sometimes all it takes to see something new in Scripture is to stare at the words from new angles, like rearranging letters in a game of Scrabble to see new words to spell. That was the technique used in this chapter regarding the keyword *neighbor*.

Psalm 111:10; Proverbs 1:7; and Proverbs 9:10 all share the famous thought that the fear of God is the beginning of wisdom. We typically concentrate on the word *wisdom*. What new insights come if you look at these verses from the angle of the word *beginning* instead? Try reading the verses aloud and vocally emphasizing the word *beginning* more than the word *wisdom* to jump-start your thought process. Follow it until you, with the Lord's help, see something new. After you come up with your own ideas, check out what I discovered on dougnewton.com or the Fresh Eyes app.

5

EMANATIONS OF GOD

The Kingdom Is Within

Luke 17:21

There is a way out of common depression
and sadness, but it isn't through
the pursuit of your happiness.

Picture this: a husband comes home from a long workday. Maybe it's the way he tosses the keys on the counter or doesn't look at his wife when she says "Hi." Or maybe he says "Hi" but his tone, even in just one syllable, says it all. He's frustrated.

Yet he doesn't need to explain his frustration. His wife already knows: it's that issue with his boss ... again. Same old thing: no gratitude for all his long extra hours. So she walks over to him and simply touches his hand. No words. She knows he isn't interested in talking. Her touch is sufficient.

And she's right. That touch was just enough to help him come all the way home. He lifts his head and turns toward her; his eyes brighten a bit as he manages a genuine "And how was your day?"

Isn't it amazing how much two persons can communicate without words? Animals give off pheromones—fragrances that send signals—but we human beings seem to give off much more complex signals. Scientists who study facial signals tell us that the face is amazingly articulate. It can convey more than 150 emotions, and the average person learns from child-hood how to read these expressions.[1]

The longer we live with others, the better we learn to "read" their unspoken messages, what we might call *emanations*—outward evidence of inner emotions. More than that, neuroscientists also assert that human beings possess a natural capacity not only to detect but also mirror others' emotions. This capacity makes empathy possible—feeling the feelings of others. Simply put, people around us can often tell and even feel what's going on inside us.

We *emanate*.

Consequently, the minute the husband walked in the door, he didn't need to say anything. His wife *knew* what he was feeling. She *sensed* not just his physical presence but his emotional presence as well. This is what people can do, and that leads to something you may never have noticed about Jesus' statement that the "kingdom of God is within" us (Luke 17:21 KJV).

It would take a whole book—indeed, a whole library of books have been written—to try to define what Jesus meant by *kingdom of God*. Rather than showing you some new meaning, I hope to share a new implication, a wonderful benefit that comes from the fact that God's kingdom is inside you. This new insight also helps solve one of the most disappointing problems many Christians encounter in their faith: the lack of the peace and joy the Bible claims they should be experiencing.

GOD THE PERSON

Although it is often a neglected and underappreciated trait of the Holy Spirit, God's Spirit is a person. Orthodox theology refers to Him as the "third person" of the Trinity. Of course, we must take great care when we think about God as a person, because there is undoubtedly more to His personhood than ours. He is infinitely more than we are in every way. Yet qualitatively we share many traits with Him simply because we are also persons. So for example, the earthly life of Jesus, who was and is the "exact representation of [His] being" (Heb. 1:3), showed us that God experiences a full range of emotions such as joy and grief, rage and relief—though always holy and pure, of course. Those emotions are part of personhood.

Therefore, it is not incorrect for us to conclude that God, as a true person, brings with Him wherever He goes "emanations" of His personhood. If a wife can detect the emanations of her husband's personhood when he walks in the door, human beings should be able to detect the Divine Person's emanations when He is near.

There is one difference, however, between the wife detecting her husband and us detecting God. The wife's experience of her husband is based on his emanations coming to her from *outside* herself. Our experience of God is based on His emanations coming to us from *inside* ourselves. That's because the person of God's Spirit dwells within every believer. In other words, to say the kingdom of God is within us means we should be able to feel God's feelings.

Something the apostle Paul wrote to the Roman believers seems to support that preliminary conclusion: "For the kingdom of God is not a matter of eating and drinking, but of righteousness, peace and joy in the Holy Spirit" (Rom. 14:17). If peace and joy in the Holy Spirit are realities in the kingdom of God and if the kingdom of God is within every believer, then our sensations of peace and joy are the result of the emanation of God's peace and joy within us. I believe that is a simple but biblical way of understanding what we mean when we talk about "sensing God's presence." We are experiencing the emanations of God the Person in our spirits. If that is the case, then we ought to think carefully about what would trigger God the Person's emotions.

GOD, THE PERSON INSIDE

Picture it this way. When you became a Christian, God took up residence inside you, as if He was in your internal living room, the heart of your home. As you go through life, He's within you, reacting to your decisions and actions, just as the husband in our opening scenario reacted to his boss.

Most of the time you don't "sense" God's presence, because His reactions are minimal. Your life, being relatively routine, is nothing to get excited about one way or another. But what if you make a choice that flatly contradicts God's expressed will? What if, for example, you lie to your spouse about a purchase you shouldn't have made? Or what if in frustration you speak demeaning words to him or her? According to Scripture, those actions will actually grieve God's Spirit (Eph. 4:30). That is, He will react negatively with some degree of frustration. Picture Him stirring within: "No, no, no! I've been over this with you a hundred times. I've told you, 'Don't hide purchases from your wife with lies'" or "I can't believe you did it again. I've told you, 'Don't make her feel put down by your criticism.'"

Guess what? That "grief" is an emanation from God's Spirit you are bound to sense. Of course, that's not the kind of "sensing God's presence" anyone hopes for.

But imagine this: one day a neighbor comes over to your house to tell you about a rumor going around about your family. He tells you who's spreading it, and now you have the option to be angry and say something biting against the gossiper. *After all*, you think, *if they're saying something evil about my family, why should I be kind about them?*

But then you remember the Bible's instruction to bless people who mistreat us, even when they speak evil against us (Luke 6:28). And "Do not let any unwholesome talk come out of your mouths" (Eph. 4:29). So you resolve, *I will say nothing unkind but try to be gracious by God, my great help.*

At that moment, you may sense God's Spirit within you excitedly congratulating and encouraging you. This amazing person inside you responds to your decision to do what is right and call for His help, emanating sheer delight. You will experience His pleasure internally.

Is this oversimplifying the spiritual experience? Of course. But with complex realities, oversimplification is a great place to start. I see no reason to clutter up the picture with something too complicated before we acknowledge simple truths. God is a person who dwells inside His people and who reacts to our choices. Why should we not take His reactions to our choices as primarily what we call "sensing the presence of God"?

SHARING GOD'S HAPPINESS

In fact, here's how it works. Since the Bible declares God is the source of life and all good things (James 1:17), any experience of true joy must have its source in God. Therefore, since God the Source dwells in you by His Spirit, your experience of joy must be emanating from God's experience of joy. The simple answer to the question of how peace and joy happen in our lives is this: if the God who dwells in you is pleased and full of joy, you will be too. Does that not align with what the Bible says elsewhere? "The joy *of* the LORD is your strength" (Neh. 8:10).

It does not say, "Your joy *about* the LORD is your strength." It's God's joy in you that makes you strong.

If that is the case, one question naturally follows. What kinds of choices stand the best chance of eliciting a joyful response from God? What choices make God satisfied and content, leaving you feeling His peace? Obviously, any obedient act will please God. Here are four verses that underscore that fact and validate our attributing humanlike emotions of pleasure to God.

- "The one who sent me is with me; he has not left me alone, for I always do what *pleases* him" (John 8:29).

- "Live as children of light (for the fruit of the light consists in all goodness, righteousness and truth) and find out what *pleases* the Lord" (Eph. 5:8–10).

- "Children, obey your parents in everything, for this *pleases* the Lord" (Col. 3:20).

- "I urge, then, first of all, that petitions, prayers, intercession and thanksgiving be made for all people—for kings and all those in authority, that we may live peaceful and quiet lives in all godliness and holiness. This is good, and *pleases* God our Savior" (1 Tim. 2:1–3).

Our obedience creates pleasure in God. But one more place in Scripture affirms my argument and directs our attention to the best way to please God and experience His peace and joy in the Holy Spirit. It's the famous parable of the talents that includes this well-known, twice-spoken statement often quoted at funerals: "Well done, good and faithful servant! You have been faithful with a few things; I will put you in charge of many things. Come and share your master's happiness!" (Matt. 25:21, 23).

While this parable is usually misunderstood (I explain how in *Fresh Eyes on Jesus' Parables*), right now we should notice that last sentence for the way it underscores my claims in this chapter.

First, what we do can make God happy. The Greek word used in this passage is the word for "joy." The faithful servants' efforts made the master joyful. We must be careful not to automatically equate the master or king figure in a parable with God. That doesn't always work. But in this parable it does.

Second—and this is confirming and exciting—God wants us to experience His joy. In the original Greek, the sentence reads, "Enter the joy of your master." God's heart's desire is that His servants faithfully work to profit His kingdom, and when they do, He invites them to experience His joy. This gives us hope but also presents a sobering diagnostic question: If a Christian's experience of peace and joy comes from the joyful emanations of God prompted by our faithful and fruitful service, then what might the lack of joy and peace suggest?

ENJOYING JOY AGAIN

If you have been following the argument so far, then that question is not hard to answer. Under ordinary circumstances, the lack of joy and peace means a person is not "making God happy" in some way because of their choices and actions. This is the place to begin looking when a person experiences common depression. (Of course, there are forms of depression that are severe and based in physiological or psychological disorders or trauma, but I am talking about common depression and anxiety that cloud many people's lives.) If this is the case, then there are generally two biblical courses of action.

Inspection

Ask God to examine your heart, mind, and life for any evidence of sin. The psalmist urged us to pray, "Search me, God.... See if there is any offensive way in me" (Ps. 139:23–24). You probably know those verses well, but be very careful. Often Christians try to engage in *self*-examination. But we do not have a search warrant. Only God does. It is not our place to look for errant ways in heart or mind without the light of His wisdom. We can't know our inner workings. Too many false impressions and strong compulsions for self-protection make us very poor examiners. However, when we faithfully leave ourselves open to God's inspection, we can trust Him to reveal "offensive" ways when we need to see them.

If you lack peace and joy, humble yourself before the Lord and ask Him to show you where your heart has gone offtrack. Here's what you will find. When you see and confess where you went wrong, the joy of the Lord will begin to rise up in you even before you have a chance to change your behavior. Why? Because God the Person in you is thrilled that you have come to Him for correction.

Circumspection

Unlike inspection, which only the Lord should undertake, circumspection is partly your responsibility, because it involves actions you can observe rather than heart matters you can't. You can hear the words you speak and see the choices you make. Those are open for evaluation. In this regard, the primary question to ask yourself is whether you are engaging in the acts of service and compassion that conform to the ways of God's kingdom. When you engage in kingdom work as a life priority, everything else you need, including any joy or peace you lack, is added to your life (Matt. 6:33).

Even nonbelievers experience this kingdom benefit. Many psychological studies have shown that meaningful, sacrificial service can provide a powerful antidote to common depression.[2] The Lord is so good He pours sunshine and showers blessings on the righteous and the unrighteous (Matt. 5:45). However, the great benefit for believers is that these blessings occur internally as the joy of the Lord springs up from within (John 7:38–39).

If you believe this and genuinely pursue pleasing God as your first priority, you will experience fewer days when you come home from work or other activities emanating frustration and discontent. Wouldn't that be a blessing for you and everyone around you!

20/20 FOCUS

1. Sometimes we worry about connecting human personhood with divine personhood. While we must take care when making that kind of correlation, can you recall places where Jesus gave us permission to think about God having traits like us?

2. This chapter presents a fresh way to think about what it means to sense God's presence. Can you put that new perspective into your own words?

What was a situation when you experienced an inner "emanation" of God?

3. Have you ever struggled with common depression or some degree of persistent discouragement? How did it lift? Did you ever notice a correlation between engaging in acts of meaningful service to others and a decrease in feelings of depression or discouragement? Is it possible you were experiencing an inner "rush" of God's pleasure?

Lord, I would like to feel happier than I do most of the time. But I don't think my happiness should depend on circumstances going my way. I'd like to feel a deep kind of happiness—or call it joy—even when times are tough. This chapter made me realize that, paradoxically, joy comes when I seek Your happiness, not my own. So I ask for life, liberty, and the pursuit of Your happiness. I trust that even this prayer pleases You. Amen.

VISION CHECK

New Scripture insights often come when we make logical analogies as this chapter does. If what we mean by the term *person* includes emotions, and God is a person, then He must have emotions. And if one person can often sense another person's emotions, then we should be able to sense God's emotions when we are in His presence. This skill of using analogies must be practiced, but it can increase over time.

To practice, go to Psalm 23:1–4, which compares the Lord to a shepherd and describes what a shepherd does for the sheep. However, it says little about what the sheep do. Think about the role and activity, if any, the sheep have in the process of being shepherded and begin making connections between sheep and people. What implications do you discover from this analogy? Jot down your thoughts and then go to dougnewton.com or the Fresh Eyes app to see what I came up with.

6

THE BURDEN OF BUSYNESS

Come, All Who Are Weary

Matthew 11:28–30

If you live on the edge of exhaustion, *don't*
try to fix it the way the world advises.

As incredible as it may seem, what may be America's biggest social problem today is something the Bible never forecasted. We probably have several nominees vying for the top spot. Drug and alcohol addiction, racism, gun violence, poverty, sexual abuse, divorce, and abortion seem to be front-runners. But I think a serious yet often-overlooked problem is *busyness.*

On the surface, busyness seems innocuous, nothing more than a bothersome pest we try to swat away: "Oh yeah, I wish I wasn't so busy, but that's just the way things are right now." However, busyness is not harmless. It does violence to marriages and families. It assaults our spirits and batters our emotions. It causes broken promises and frayed nerves. All the good things in life that bring peace and contentment require time that busyness steals away.

If you asked me, "What is the biggest change you have seen in the church over your forty-plus years of pastoral ministry?" I would answer, "People have gotten so busy it's hard to be a healthy church anymore." What could be more detrimental to the world than the loss of healthy churches? Something has gone dangerously wrong when participation in the body of Christ—one of the Christian's key callings—becomes one of many secondary "events" that has to be squeezed into the family itinerary between soccer games and dance lessons.

You would think if *busyness* was such a huge problem, the Bible would say a lot about it. But surprise … the Bible says nothing. Scour the pages of Scripture from beginning to end and you won't find a thing about the problem of being too busy. Oh, it uses the word *busy* a few times: "For the fool speaks folly, and his heart is busy with iniquity" (Isa. 32:6 ESV). "We hear that some among you are idle and disruptive. They are not busy; they are busybodies" (2 Thess. 3:11). But none of these addresses the problem we call busyness: being over-committed, running around helter-skelter, having no time for sit-down family meals, struggling to keep all the plates spinning. The surprising and sobering fact is that this huge problem did not exist for most people during the centuries in which the Bible was written. This problem is unprecedented. "Stop and smell the roses" is not a Bible saying.

It's arguable whether people are as busy as they claim. Being "busy" is a status symbol, it seems, so people like to think of themselves as busy. However, regardless of what a time-management study would reveal, everyone feels rushed and ragged. We clamor for more sleep, because we feel so tired. We jump at the latest time-saving schemes. We can now control and monitor our home lighting, heating, and security through our cell phones, an ability that is becoming more important because we are never home to flip switches and lock doors. Ironically, all these time-saving methods and devices allow us to cram our mobile lives with more activity, not less. Feelings of frustration and fragmentation mount, because our days are full of scattered pieces that don't hold together thematically.

At this point, we cast about looking for solutions to feeling overwhelmed and tired. The obvious answer, it seems, is to figure out a way to scale back our activities. We devour books about "simplifying." We commiserate with friends and agree to create margin or boundaries. We think, *That's what I need to do. After all, I'm no good to anybody else if I'm not taking care of myself.* We resign from committees or groups we didn't really want to participate in anyway. For about two weeks we enjoy a little relief from feeling overwhelmed. But human nature abhors a vacuum, and before long we've let ourselves get overloaded again. Our time is like money; when we save it in one place, we tend to spend it in another.

Attempting to relieve the burden of busyness by trying to slow down, simplify, and create margin is like scooping out a hole in the sand at the seashore. The next wave fills it back in. We need to do something different. That's where this famous saying of the Lord, which promises rest for burdened and weary people, comes in. It presents us with a solution, but it's so countercultural and counterintuitive most people miss it.

A COUNTERCULTURAL SOLUTION

We must never underestimate the influence of the technological culture that surrounds us. It's the air we breathe. Without our noticing, it trains us to view life according to a push-button paradigm. That is, we approach everything as a problem to be fixed, a need to be met, or a desire to be satisfied, as though we only need to find the right pill, the right routine, the right relationship, or the right opportunity and everything will work out. Most of us have developed a deeply ingrained habit of relying on things outside ourselves and, ironically, within ourselves to figure out how to *possess* those things we want most. If only we can figure it all out before it's too late.

However, Jesus' famous promise about "soul rest" begins with one habit-breaking requirement: "Come to me" (Matt. 11:28). We read right past that requirement without pausing to recognize its embedded challenge. It implies that there is no hope for soul rest by going to any other source of help. Again, you might be nodding your head as if that point is obvious. And it may be, intellectually. But the ways we fail to act according to that fundamental principle may not be so obvious.

The famous Psalm 23 begins by stating, "The LORD is my shepherd" (v. 1). It then talks about green pastures and quiet waters where a person can find rest, refreshment, and guidance (vv. 2–3). But the most important word in those verses is the pronoun *he*. "*He* makes me lie down" (v. 2). "*He* leads me" (v. 2).

"*He* refreshes my soul" (v. 3). "*He* guides me" (v. 3). All these soul-satisfying provisions come because of the Shepherd Lord.

However, if we look at our lives honestly, too much of the time we live as if "I am my shepherd." I am looking for green pastures. I am searching for quiet waters. I am taking on the responsibility for restoration. If I am going to relieve this burden of busyness that so wearies me, I will have to take matters into my own hands. Figure it out. Come up with a new game plan. Scale back my activities. Learn to say no.

In stark contrast, Jesus' promise of soul rest begins with a 180-degree shift away from the cultural habit of figuring things out on our own. No matter how convincing or compelling the advice other sources give us, it is not our domain to make these decisions. We need boundaries against burnout. Yes. But we do not set them. He does. We need time for personal space, but we do not schedule it at our own discretion. And yes, we need breathers—green pastures and still waters. We can't handle non-stop service. But the Lord is our shepherd, not we ourselves. He knows when. He knows what and how much. When we try to work out self-care in our own wisdom to guarantee rest and restoration, we inevitably fall into the category of those who are trying to "save their life." This always backfires (Luke 9:24).

Just as God led the Israelites out of bondage in Egypt, the only way out of the burden of busyness is to be guided out by the Lord. That brings us to the counterintuitive part of this promise of soul rest.

A COUNTERINTUITIVE SOLUTION

As we have already seen, when we try to be our own shepherds, our natural path to rest involves slowing down, backing out of commitments, and learning to say no. But according to Jesus' invitation to come to Him, rest comes through doing work. Read that again: according to Jesus, rest comes through doing work! (If you are panicking right now, take a deep breath and stick with me.)

This is counterintuitive. You would think rest comes from laying off work. However, notice what Jesus says right after the promise "I will give you rest" (Matt. 11:28). He says, "Take my yoke upon you" (v. 29). Over the years, I've heard many teachers explain how the yoke works, and it's very interesting. But ironically the main point gets lost in the detailed explanation. It's lying right on the surface: a yoke symbolizes work, even hard work. You don't take on a yoke to sit on the couch. You don't find soul rest by looking for ways to relax. You look for ways to do work—just a special kind of work. You join Jesus in *His* work. But I am not talking about "the Lord's work" in a generic sense. Lots of people get exhausted doing the Lord's work, generally speaking. They live their Christian lives as if there's a to-do list from here to kingdom come—literally.

Jesus' yoke differs from that. There may be a thousand things we could do that fall into the category of "the Lord's work," but on any given day or during any given season, the Lord is saying something more specific: "Work with Me on *this*." Listening for those more specific instructions, finding that personal yoke, is the only kind of work, the only thing, that will bring soul rest. And it really does ... even when you're bone tired physically.

A few years ago, I was leading a midweek small group. One night the end of the meeting neared, and we generally closed our group meeting with an open time of prayer. On this night I was tired and hoping the prayer time would be short. I was more eager to get home, kick up my feet, and watch a favorite TV program than I was to "pray for one another." However, during this time in my life I was learning how to sense the Lord's prompting toward specific prayer. So even though I was not in an enthusiastic "listening" mode at that moment, I did unfortunately "hear" something in my mind that aroused my attention: "Say to her, 'Susan, you were a good child.'"

The thought came out of the blue, and it did not seem fitting for what I knew about Sue. Plus, it seemed like a strange thing to say to a person in that setting. So I faced a decision. Should I act on the thought or pass it off as bogus so I could get home to my comfy clothes and bag of chips? Probably driven more by potential guilt than spiritual vigor, I interrupted the prayer time and tentatively delivered the message. "Sue, I think I'm supposed to tell you that you were a good child." And I'm glad I did.

The second I said the words, Sue and her husband wept with tears of joy and freedom. After composing themselves, they explained what was going on. Without going into the somewhat-chilling details, unknown to me or anyone in the group, this couple had been going through a very hard time. Over the previous months they had experienced some traumatic moments that led to Sue seeking counseling. The counselor tracked some of her problems back to childhood issues related to her dad and her parents' divorce.

The counselor had assigned Sue to write a letter to herself as a child to tell her child-self, from her adult point of view, that she was a good child. That very afternoon before our group meeting, she sat at her kitchen table with a blank sheet of paper, trying to complete the counselor's assignment, but she couldn't. Sobbing, she told her husband, "I can't do it because I wasn't good! I wasn't good!"

So when I spoke those words—words I couldn't have known to say—Sue and her husband were enabled to embrace the liberating truth she struggled to accept, because the message clearly came from the Lord. And me? It didn't matter whether I got home to get some rest, because my soul was restored. I had the thrill of working alongside the Lord. *Wow, His yoke was light!*

These kinds of situations don't happen every day. But their impact lingers. Plus, they can happen frequently enough to keep us living consistently in that paradox of soul rest through yoke work.

HOW TO STEP UNDER THE YOKE

People wonder how to stay in a listening posture so they hear these kinds of "yoke" instructions from the Lord. The fundamental answer is to "remain" in the Lord through prayer and immersion in His Word. But I have found an additional, more specific habit to develop that keeps us sensitized to God's voice. Live a permission-seeking life.

When you bring the Lord into the loop of all your decisions, not just the major ones you worry about, your ability to perceive God's voice increases. However, so often we don't even think to ask the Lord for permission before we act, because we tend to assume if something is not morally wrong, it is automatically right, as if it comes with built-in permission. That is not true. We must develop the habit of consulting the Lord to give Him opportunity to speak into every situation. "Lord, there is nothing inherently wrong about spending our money to take a relaxing trip to the mountains, but is that okay with You?" Initially, the act of pausing to include the Lord before simple decisions may seem artificial and even unnecessary, but that habit develops spiritual sensitivity.

My wife, Margie, and I have been married forty-three years. I know her very well—what she likes, doesn't like, values, and doesn't value. If we played the Oldywed Game (rather than the Newlywed Game), I would probably guess her answers correctly every time. Paradoxically, however, the longer I have loved and trusted her and the more I know about her heart and mind, the less likely I am to make decisions without getting her input first. That's what love and respect create: a passion to keep the loved one in the loop.

Don't assume you know what the Lord wants you to do without asking. In our Christian subculture, we are often told that having a passion for something good, plus the personal gifts and strengths to accomplish it, is how you discern God's will. After all, He wouldn't have made you with those passions and gifts if He didn't want you doing those things. Yet even this is not necessarily true. Something can be good, you can be gifted and even feel called, but you still should seek God's permission before you act. You may not be the person He wants to use in that situation, this may not be the time to act, or you may not be ready. In other words, never assume you have God's permission until you explicitly seek it. When this becomes your habit, your listening skills increase.

So don't quit everything, buy a small farm in South Dakota, and raise chickens, thinking you'll fix the problem of busyness—unless He tells you to. You can find green pastures right where you are. Jesus, your Shepherd, is inviting you to off-load your heavy burden of busyness, accept the easy burden of His daily business, and the rest—as promised—will follow.

20/20 FOCUS

1. State in your own words the common advice the world gives to people who are overwhelmed by busyness.

2. In what ways have you attempted to follow the world's advice or tried to be your own shepherd? (Be as honest as possible.)

3. Make a list of some of the good things you have been doing but which the Lord may not have directed you to do.

4. Is there something you have sensed, perhaps for a long time, that the Lord has been wanting you to do but other good things have kept you too busy?

Lord, I am tired of being tired. I've been relating to You all wrong. I've been asking You to step under my yoke to help me pull my load, rather than stepping under Your yoke to join Your work. I want that to change, but I'm scared I won't

recognize Your voice and I'll just start taking on
more things I can't handle. I really need rest—true
spiritual rest. So I'm ready to listen and do only
what You tell me. Help me trust You to show me
Your yoke. Amen.

VISION CHECK

Almost everything Jesus said or did was counter to the common ways of thinking and acting, as seen in this chapter about the way true rest comes through divinely directed work. One way to discover something new in Scripture is to expect to find principles and perspectives that are upside down or backward in relation to conventional thinking. Start by writing down a sentence that captures conventional wisdom. Then ask yourself, *What if that is not the right way to look at things?* and imagine the exact opposite.

Try this: a common assumption among Christians is that we are supposed to be about the Lord's work. That's our calling: to be doing the Lord's work. But what if, in one sense, that's not the case? Read two portions of Scripture (John 1:19–34; 3:22–30) that describe John the Baptist's work and expect to see things differently from what conventional thinking would suggest. Write down your ideas. Then go to dougnewton.com or the Fresh Eyes app to see what I saw.

7

GOOD IMPRESSIONS

My Ways Are Not Yours
Isaiah 55:8–9

Wouldn't it be nice if we could know
what God was thinking and doing?

I've accidentally ruined a few things in my life. Like the time I decided to repair our 1971 Volkswagen van with the help of *Volkswagen Repair for Dummies*. Apparently I should have purchased the coloring-book version, *Volkswagen Repair for Ultra Dummies*.

Then there was the time we installed new carpet in our bedroom. After doing that, the doors wouldn't open, of course. Because of the carpet's extra height, there was not enough gap between the floor and the bottom of the door. So I took the door off the hinges, carried it out to the garage, laid it on two sawhorses, marked a line where I would cut off a half inch, and set up a guide rail to make sure the line was straight and smooth. Proud of myself, I thought, *That's just like Dad would have done it.*

Unfortunately, Dad was not there to head me off at the pass. When I laid the door across the sawhorses, I noticed a gash on the face of the door. *Might as well cut that end and get rid of the unsightly scratch*, I thought. I did everything right—safety glasses, perfect cut, remounted it on the hinges, dropped the hinge pins in—and realized it still dragged on the carpet … because I had cut the wrong end. There was now a huge half-inch gap between the top of the door and the doorframe. Smart? No.

I could keep describing other ruinous mistakes I have made. Perhaps you've accidentally wrecked some things too—and if you would send me an email, it would make me feel better. Sometimes those ruinous mistakes prove more costly than comical. Such is the case with the famous saying about God's higher ways and thoughts highlighted in this chapter. No one set out to mess up this text, but the standard application has caused harmful effects.

Over my years of pastoral ministry, I have found most people come out of the spiritual starting gate with a preformed view of God as distant and austere. Then they hear these two verses as reminders of how different and far above us God is. I've even heard the text read with a stern voice and an index finger striking the air percussively: "For *my* thoughts are *not your* thoughts …" The preacher's tone of voice seems to add, "And don't you forget it!" The passage continues, "'Neither are your ways my ways,' declares the LORD. 'As the heavens are higher than the earth, so are my ways *higher than your ways* and my thoughts than your thoughts'" (Isa. 55:8–9).

That unfortunate view of God's distant otherness increases our struggle to view Him as approachable. We hear, "Warning! Watch your attitude! Know your place. He is God. You are not!" Even if Bible teachers didn't sound so harsh, their point was still that God is not like us. He is totally "other" than we. The things going on in His holy heart and His genius mind are vastly superior to the things going on in ours morally and intellectually. So don't expect to discern His ways and understand His thoughts.

But is this really what this passage is saying to us?
What about sayings like Corinthians
Poses the ? - how do we reconcile those to characteristics: 1) Holy

BY INVITATION ONLY *Otherness, or 2) Gods desire to be One w/us?*

It is important that
We understand the motive behind this kind of "otherness" talk. With succinctness, it keeps our heads bowed and hearts humble. The problem is that this idea of God's otherness—while true—is not the point of the chapter within which these verses *So what is it about?* are found. In fact, the chapter teaches quite the opposite. It is all about the Totally Other One wanting to bridge the unbridgeable gulf between us. *Hopefully---* You'll see that more clearly after noting four observations.

Observation 1: notice the striking rapid succession of *of the 1st 6 verses...* imperative verbs in the opening. An imperative verb gives a command of some sort. Some commands are pushy, but others are pleasant, because they act as invitations. That's what we read here. The first six verses contain fifteen invitations; I've put them in italics: "*Come*, all you who are thirsty, *come* to the waters; and you who have no money, *come*, *buy* and *eat*! *Come*, *buy* wine and milk without money and without cost. Why spend money on what is not bread, and your labor on what does not satisfy? *Listen*, *listen* to me, and *eat* what is good, and you will delight in the richest of fare. *Give ear* and *come* to me; *listen*, that you may live…. *Seek* the LORD while he may be found; *call* on him while he is near" (Isa. 55:1–3, 6). *Are you beginning to see the context?*

Does this sound like someone who wants to keep His distance? Is His point to make sure we remember how far removed He is from us? *Uniqueness of Christianity … God initiated pursue*

Observation 2: To whom is God extending all these gracious invitations? What is their condition? They are penniless. They are identified as those "who have no money" (v. 1)—people *of Bang* who lack the ability or resources to get what they need. *Parable*

Observation 3: What is He offering these people? Wine, milk, and bread that can be bought in a figurative sense, because they are offered "without cost" (v. 1). It is important to note that God is inviting them to more than a soup line of basic sustenance. His invitation includes a banquet table spread with the "richest of fare" (v. 2). *God of Abundance! No Lack!*

Observation 4: What will result if people accept His invitation? The rich fare is symbolic. The cuisine God offers delights the soul, not just the palate, and gives life (v. 3). *I have food that you know not of … to do*

The context of this famous saying is God offering rich spiri- *the will of my Father* tual food to people who have no resources or ability to obtain it—even encouraging them to come enjoy it. That being the case, we must approach the "higher ways and thoughts" verses not *just* as a warning but as an invitation as well. Here God invites human beings to receive, drink, and eat His life-giving and life-delighting thoughts and ways—thoughts and ways that are far

[handwritten note: Jesus Great Invitation "Come unto me..."]

above and beyond our own. The whole point of the chapter is not for us to be afraid to come and get this greater "food" from Him *or* even to encourage our humility before God! The context totally destroys the common idea that these verses tell us what we *can't* know. In fact, in stark contrast, they declare the heights of what we *can* know, if we'll only come and seek.

[handwritten note: Biblical Idea of Humility "Broken w/o God"]

RAIN IN THE FORECAST

How do we draw near to obtain His thoughts if they are so high above ours? Do we try to meditate our way up, to some state of heavenly consciousness? No! God bridges the unbridge-able distance by sending His thoughts and ways to us. He told His people, "As the heavens are higher than the earth, so are my ways higher than your ways and my thoughts than your thoughts. As the rain and the snow come down from heaven, and do not return to it without watering the earth … so is my word that goes out from my mouth" (vv. 9–11).

[handwritten note: But biblical meditation is encouraged]

[handwritten note: Word Centered life... We are what we eat!]

The parallels in verses 9 and 10 establish that the starting loca-tion of God's thoughts is the starting location of rain and snow and that the rain coming down to produce buds, seeds, and bread is like God's words. They come from heaven out of His mouth to produce and promote His will on earth. God promised, "So is my word that goes out from my mouth: It will not return to me empty, but will accomplish what I desire and achieve the purpose for which I sent it" (v. 11). God sends words from heaven that express and enact His ways and thoughts to those who come, buy, eat, listen, delight, seek, and call, according to His invitation.

But this promising invitation comes with one condition and prerequisite: "Let the wicked forsake their ways and the unrighteous their thoughts" (v. 7). It is simply logical that before we should expect to receive what God has to offer, we must clear away the clutter of our own ways and thoughts. Once we have done that, then the rest is up to God. God continuously showers the earth with His ways and thoughts, and they are free to anyone who responds to His invitation. But don't we already have this "food" from God in His Word?

Do We Really Believe this?

Saved when Believe
Forgiven when Repent
Pray when Confess
Answers when Ask
Find when Seek
Doors Open when knock

THE DANGER ZONE

God already deposited His thoughts and showed us His ways in Holy Scripture. *I want us to think about something...* His written Word provides an inexhaustible storehouse of spiritual food. In its pages, we meet the Spirit of God and find life, as Isaiah 55 promises. But the gift of God's ways and thoughts is not exclusively there. *The Word is the written expression of who He is!*

Jesus is the living expression

The clearest and best revelation comes in the person of Jesus Christ, the way, the truth, and the life. As we know from John's gospel, He is the very Word of God made flesh and the bread of life (1:14; 6:35). Jesus embodied the invitation of Isaiah 55 and its fulfillment.

Moved... compelled y. led to... feel like...
God to told me to..

But God also deposits His thoughts *directly into our minds*. Our thoughts actually often are His thoughts. This is the third and often-neglected location where the raindrops of God's ways and thoughts land. It's neglected because of the well-known dangers involved in making assumptions in this area. Much damage has been done by people who claim to have a "word from God" or an "impression" that is way off base. Yet rather than steer clear, we should learn to steer carefully.

Scripture provides a great deal of evidence that God wants to deposit His thoughts directly into our minds. Scripture explicitly states that happened for many of the Old Testament prophets (Isaiah, Jeremiah, and Ezekiel, for example). Since Pentecost, ordinary people also enjoy this privilege, according to Acts 2:17–18. Paul claimed we have the mind of Christ so that what we cannot conceive will be revealed to us in words the Spirit teaches (1 Cor. 2:9–16). Our responsibility is to let the Spirit control our minds. When we do so, God's words remain in us and the Spirit helps us pray when we don't know what to say. He even gives us words in challenging situations and wisdom when we ask (Matt. 10:19–20; James 1:5). The Bible says God's mind and our minds can be in much greater union than we often think.

The Old Testament prophets foretold a kind of union with God wherein His will moves our wills (Ezek. 36:26–27; Jer. 24:7). Jesus often spoke of the possibility of spiritual union with Him (e.g., John 15), and the apostle Paul reaffirmed it several times (e.g., Col. 1:27; Gal. 2:20; Rom. 8:9–11). Paul also stated that Christ is living and working in us "to will and to act in order to fulfill his good purpose" (Phil. 2:13). God obviously desires union with His people.

So here's a question: Does this spiritual union mean God moves only our wills? Does it not also mean His heart moves our hearts and His mind moves our minds? Of course. There are things He wants us to know, but there are also things He wants us to do, to join Him in, so we can be informed and instructed in His ways and thoughts all the more.

A CASE IN POINT

One day a fellow came into my church office on the brink of suicide. He was an ex-con whose wife of twenty-seven years had just announced her decision to divorce him. She could no longer handle his chronic lying that year after year led to innumerable tall tales and serious crimes. But he was also a "good guy" who had served his country in the navy. This Jekyll-Hyde moral split in his character had become unbearable to her—and now to him as well. He wanted to end it all.

I had never met him before, so I spent some time learning his story. Our conversation seemed to stabilize him for the time being. Eventually I offered to pray and asked him to come back the next day to see me at the same time, hoping an appointment of that sort would give him a reason not to take suicidal action when he left.

The next day he returned. I was relieved, and we talked some more. He did not have a personal relationship with Jesus Christ, so once again near the end of an hour I asked if I could pray with him. He agreed, and I began. I was no more than two sentences into my prayer before a thought sprang to my mind—dare I say "a strong impression"—to ask him to do something.

"Jim, I don't know why, but I think the Lord wants me to ask you to stop at a store tonight on your way home and pick up a brand-new notebook, one of those 'composition' types, and a brand new pen. I'm not sure why, but it may be the Lord wants you to document some of your costlier lies and to seek specific forgiveness from Him and the people you might have deceived. Are you willing to do that?"

I barely finished before, with an astonished look, he jumped in. He said, "When I left here yesterday, I stopped at the store to pick up milk and was walking past the school supplies section. I had the strongest compulsion to go down the aisle. I didn't know why. Then I saw the section with notebooks"—he reached for the backpack he had brought—"and I bought a new notebook. Then I thought I should get a new pen. So I did. And I brought them with me today." As he was explaining, he pulled out the new pen and composition notebook and placed them on the table in front of us!

Now we were both astonished, but I gathered myself enough to say, "Jim, you see? God is letting you know that He wants to save your life—not just physically but spiritually."

That was several years ago, and since that time, Jim has grown spiritually. His marriage was restored and now thrives. And though he has faced serious physical problems, taking him to the brink of death several times, his faith and Christian witness are vibrant.

I can't think of any better reason for God to want His ways and thoughts to rain down on people like us—who are not nearly wise or holy enough to handle situations like Jim's—so the world around us would have a chance to know God is real and close at hand. Lord, forgive us for misusing this famous saying as a warning to humble us rather than an invitation to nourish and employ us.

20/20 FOCUS

1. For some reason many, many Christians seem inclined to see God as distant and austere—as if He's unapproachable and ready to zap us if we become too familiar. Why do you think that is?

2. This chapter focuses attention on the indisputable spirit of invitation in Isaiah 55. Can you think of other passages in Scripture that similarly encourage people to accept an invitation to connect with and receive from the Lord?

3. Most of the chapter talks about the Lord giving us His thoughts. But Isaiah 55 also promises us we'll be given His ways. What might that mean?

4. Think about some area of uncertainty or responsibility you face that requires more knowledge or wisdom than you currently have. Reconsider this passage and accept the Lord's invitation to "come, buy and eat" what you need.

Lord, the fresh insights from this Scripture open up my heart and mind to new possibilities. But my faith still feels weak. Will You really supply me with Your ways and thoughts? I want to believe that You will, especially in light of how frequently I feel at a loss about what to do or think in tough times. Help me trust You enough to reach out and receive. Help me be a living example of a person who hears and speaks Your words and walks in Your ways. Amen.

VISION CHECK

Carpenters have a rule of thumb: measure twice; cut once. In other words, double-check to make sure you're right before doing something you can't undo. We need to apply that rule to interpreting a Bible passage. Am I sure I understand the context? Check it again. Even if it seems as if there's no other way to think about it, check it again. In the time you take to check and recheck, you are giving the Lord time to show you something new.

Read Romans 7:18–19, where Paul spoke candidly about his struggle to do what's right against his sinful impulses. He said, "I know that good itself does not dwell in me, that is, in my sinful nature. For I have the desire to do what is good, but I cannot carry it out. For I do not do the good I want to do, but the evil I do not want to do—this I keep on doing." This Scripture is often used to describe Christians' inevitable struggle against our sinful natures. Is that what Paul was getting at? Double-check the context starting from the beginning of the chapter. You may even have to triple-check it. Here's the question: Was Paul referring to his present or his former condition? What do you see? Find out what I saw by going to dougnewton.com or the Fresh Eyes app.

8

THE GREATER COMMISSION

Go and Make Disciples
Matthew 28:19–20

Are you sure you're hearing the same
commission the disciples heard?

Christmas usually disappointed me as a kid. Even though I grew up in a stable Christian home with wonderful parents who invested a lot of effort in holidays like Christmas, I often felt a vague sadness at the end of Christmas Day. Yes, we had fun opening presents, and I usually got the top items on my wish list. But the way it was over so quickly—this day I had waited weeks for—left me depressed. Santa didn't deliver anything that lasted. By December 26, I had drained not only the batteries for the remote-control car I had wanted for so long but also my enthusiasm for it.

Even though Mom and Gram always baked sweet rolls, pecan pies, and sugar cookies that lasted for several days, some ingredient must've been left out of the overall holiday recipe, because Christmas itself tasted flat. *Navidad* was always less *feliz* than I hoped.

Sometimes I caused that disappointment. I snooped. One year I had to know whether I was getting the ukulele I'd begged for. Four days before Christmas I found it under my parents' bed. Couldn't their hiding place have been more creative? Christmas was spoiled. My fake surprise on Christmas morning added to my guilty feelings, and I crawled into bed that night a downcast deceiver.

As the years have gone on, I have come to accept the fact of life I first faced on those lackluster Christmases: *things rarely are all they are cracked up to be.* I am no longer disappointed about that, however. Every once in a while, the real surpasses the anticipated. Like my wife and kids. What can I say? Better dreams than you ever dreamed do sometimes come true. But most of the time the key to staving off disappointment is having realistic expectations … yet not *low* expectations.

Sadly, low expectations abound in Christian circles. *Don't have high hopes and you'll not be disappointed.* Pessimism of that sort often infiltrates our personal faith in the form of conventional wisdom. Don't expect the sense of peace to last. Don't expect to feel God's presence consistently. Don't expect to see cases of healing very often, if ever.

Like a low-grade fever that lingers and saps a person's strength, low expectations often infect otherwise potent biblical texts because of the way we interpret them. I hope to clarify this problem by looking at one of the most-quoted but most-misinterpreted Scripture texts: the so-called Great Commission. These amazing final earthly words of Jesus have been appropriately memorized but also unfortunately *vagurized.* I don't usually coin words, but there needs to be a verb for making something vague, because that's what we've done to this famous saying. And by making it vague, we have drained it of its implicit promise and power.

How have we made the Great Commission vague? By not hearing it as the disciples would have heard it, especially the part where Jesus said, "Teaching them to obey everything I have commanded you" (Matt. 28:20). We hear that command as people who now have all four gospels that include all Jesus' commands. We live almost twenty centuries down the line, with twenty centuries of church history and of scholars and practitioners who have tried to explain the disciple-making process. As a result, it's as if an eighteen-wheeler has backed up to the church's loading dock and all the discipleship experts have filled that semi with every command Jesus ever gave, every technique Jesus ever used, and every doctrine Jesus ever taught. Then in response to the question, "What do we need to teach in order to make disciples?" we ship out this truckload of discipleship commands and resources.

However, that truck delivers very little of what the disciples would have heard that day. Boxes and boxes of accumulated content Jesus never meant to include in that discipleship command cram our minds. And as we're about to see, this once "great" commission has become a gorged commission and, consequently, vague.

THE FIRST COMMISSION

Happily, we have a way of knowing—or at least making a sound assumption about—what Jesus meant and the disciples heard. How so? Scripture provides us with a parallel event, a prior commissioning moment, which Jesus referred to when He said, "Teaching them to obey everything I have commanded you." Matthew 10 records the details of what I call the First Commission, when Jesus called His first twelve disciples and gave them their marching orders. Can you imagine how memorable that moment would have been? "Jesus called his twelve disciples to him and gave them authority to drive out impure spirits and to heal every disease and sickness" (v. 1).

It is important to note two things about this verse. First, it begins by conferring authority to act in His name. That parallels the Great Commission: "All authority in heaven and on earth has been given to me. Therefore go and make disciples of all nations" (28:18–19). Second, the First Commission immediately follows Matthew's account of Jesus "healing every disease and sickness" (9:35) among the multitudes out of compassion for their "harassed and helpless" state (v. 36). This was when He looked longingly at His disciples and stated that "the harvest is plentiful but the workers are few" (v. 37) and urged them to "ask the Lord of the harvest, therefore, to send out workers into his harvest field" (v. 38).

It is crucial to see that context for the First Commission. Clearly, it reveals the deep concern and chief purpose behind the commands Jesus gave His first disciples: bring life-giving preaching and healing to the masses. That's what He was longing to see more of. So that's why He commanded them, "As you go, proclaim this message: 'The kingdom of heaven has come near.' Heal the sick, raise the dead, cleanse those who have leprosy, drive out demons. Freely you have received; freely give" (Matt. 10:7–8). These were the core *mission* commands He gave them. Until that point, His disciples had been admiring followers but still idle spectators. Imagine how surprised and even startled they might have been to hear themselves being sent out as the answer to Jesus' prayer for harvest workers.

Then Jesus added a series of *strategic* commands to follow as they fulfilled the key mission commands. We can summarize them this way: travel light, stay focused, prepare for opposition, and remain hopeful.

Travel Light Matthew 10:9–10	"Do not get any gold or silver or copper to take with you in your belts—no bag for the journey or extra shirt or sandals or a staff, for the worker is worth his keep."
Stay Focused Matthew 10:11–16	"Whatever town or village you enter, search there for some worthy person and stay at their house until you leave. As you enter the home, give it your greeting. If the home is deserving, let your peace rest on it; if it is not, let your peace return to you. If anyone will not welcome you or listen to your words, leave that home or town and shake the dust off your feet. Truly I tell you, it will be more bearable for Sodom and Gomorrah on the day of judgment than for that town. I am sending you out like sheep among wolves. Therefore, be as shrewd as snakes and as innocent as doves."

Prepare for Opposition
Matthew
10:17–25

"Be on your guard; you will be handed over to the local councils and be flogged in the synagogues. On my account you will be brought before governors and kings as witnesses to them and to the Gentiles. But when they arrest you, do not worry about what to say or how to say it. At that time you will be given what to say, for it will not be you speaking, but the Spirit of your Father speaking through you. Brother will betray brother to death, and a father his child; children will rebel against their parents and have them put to death. You will be hated by everyone because of me, but the one who stands firm to the end will be saved. When you are persecuted in one place, flee to another. Truly I tell you, you will not finish going through the towns of Israel before the Son of Man comes. The student is not above the teacher, nor a servant above his master. It is enough for students to be like their teachers, and servants like their masters. If the head of the house has been called Beelzebul, how much more the members of his household!"

Remain Hopeful
Matthew
10:26–33

"So do not be afraid of them, for there is nothing concealed that will not be disclosed, or hidden that will not be made known. What I tell you in the dark, speak in the daylight; what is whispered in your ear, proclaim from the roofs. Do not be afraid of those who kill the body but cannot kill the soul. Rather, be afraid of the One who can destroy both soul and body in hell. Are not two sparrows sold for a penny? Yet not one of them will fall to the ground outside your Father's care. And even the very hairs of your head are all numbered. So don't be afraid; you are worth more than many sparrows. Whoever acknowledges me before others, I will also acknowledge before my Father in heaven. But whoever disowns me before others, I will disown before my Father in heaven."

In summary, the First Commission contains numerous *strategic* commands associated with undertaking the five *mission* commands. Those core mission commands, in particular, would have rocked the disciples' world: "You mean we are supposed to do the works we have been watching Jesus do?" After that, the strategic commands would've added a sense of gravity to the entire commission—their obedience would be costly.

FOCUSING THE GREAT COMMISSION

Now let's return to the Great Commission and notice the ongoing parallel with the First Commission. Jesus conferred authority in both cases. Then in both cases He commanded His disciples to "go." In both He left them with words of hope, as in the Great Commission when He said, "And surely I am with you always, to the very end of the age" (Matt. 28:20). It would have seemed to the disciples as if Jesus was rewinding the tape and replaying the First Commission, except that this time they were to make disciples who obeyed the commands they had received at their initial commissioning.

Do you see it now? By uprooting the Great Commission from the context of *how* the disciples would have understood "everything I have commanded you" (v. 20), the specific commands Jesus meant are lost. We've made the Great Commission a multiplicity of commands Jesus made elsewhere but wasn't talking about here. As a result, disciple-making has become both more complicated and more vague.

In fact, the goal of disciple-making is much simpler and clearer than we tend to make it: send out disciples who fulfill the First Commission's core *mission* commands. "As you go, proclaim this message: 'The kingdom of heaven has come near.' Heal the sick, raise the dead, cleanse those who have leprosy, drive out demons. Freely you have received; freely give" (10:7–8). Sadly, in spite of all our disciple-making efforts and programs that emphasize doctrinal knowledge, kingdom values, and holy behavior, we rarely produce disciples who embrace— much less obey—these specific core commands. Of course, obeying or even attempting to obey commands like raising the dead seems inconceivable to our modern minds. Yet reputable, documented reports of such occurrences in history and around the world, such as in Craig Keener's scholarly two-volume work *Miracles*,[1] should leave us open even to that possibility.

FULFILLING THE GREAT COMMISSION

Therefore, the next logical question is this: How did Jesus develop disciples who were prepared to fulfill the First Commission? The answer once again proves disconcerting if we assume important questions always require complicated answers.

I studied philosophy in graduate school. I understand the impulse—goodness knows I fight it daily—to analyze ad absurdum. So when an answer comes along that seems too simplistic, I resist planting my feet there. However, as I face Scripture honestly, I see only three things Jesus did to shape disciples who fulfill their commission:

- *Observation:* He let them listen and watch as He lived in communion with the Father and powerfully declared and demonstrated the kingdom.

- *Impartation:* He made sure they had authority and power in His name. He both conferred it and commanded them to wait for it (Luke 24:49).

- *Delegation:* He sent them out to do what they had seen Him do—heal and deliver, both spiritually and physically, the helpless and harassed. He did not put His followers through ministry school or require proof of competence. Their task was to step out boldly and act, in on-the-job training.

How will we ever hope to fulfill the Great Commission unless we focus our attention on these basic commands Jesus gave in the First Commission? Imagine what kind of disciples we might develop and fruit we might see if we employed His simple, focused method: powerfully declare and demonstrate His kingdom, make sure disciples are filled with spiritual authority and power, and place them in front of dire human need that only the power of God can meet.

Maybe we need to *become* true disciples before we can *make* such disciples. Maybe we are followers who need the boldness to bring the kingdom ministries of healing and deliverance back into the center of the church's mission.

Have we lost confidence in what the Holy Spirit will do to enable Jesus' followers to obey Jesus' commands? Whenever that happens, human beings make things more complicated, as we substitute discipleship programs for divine power. What would happen if we appealed to the Lord, "Lord, we promise bold action if only You would release Your enabling power and authority among us again"?

Maybe my Christmases were usually less than satisfying for a similar reason. But for every disciple ready to obey Jesus' core mission commands, God has gifts just waiting to be opened that will never disappoint.

20/20 FOCUS

1. To say that our common understanding of the Great Commission is vague is not to say it is wrong or bad; it just lacks helpful specificity. How does the specificity supplied by the so-called First Commission help you?

2. What might a local church have to do in order to redesign its discipleship program to align more closely with what Jesus meant by "teaching them to obey everything I have commanded you"?

3. Notice that Jesus' "Teach them to *obey* everything …" includes commands to heal. But Jesus did not say "Teach them to *heal*." Does that make any difference in your thinking?

4. With this new understanding in mind, what are some steps you can take now to begin to fulfill the Great Commission?

Lord, I imagine You in the moment You gave the First Commission looking out over the multitudes, longing for more harvest workers. I'd love to be one of the answers to Your prayer. But wow! That's quite scary if I take the disciples' First Commission seriously as the benchmark. If You want me to do that, I'm going to need a strong sense of calling just as You gave them or I don't think I could ever step out. So here I am. Call me. Commission me. Send me. Amen.

VISION CHECK

Vagueness is the enemy of truth. Truth may sometimes be elusive, but when found, it's always crystal clear. Razor sharp. Whenever you come across a conventional teaching that leaves you wanting more specificity, don't stop with wishing. Keep searching. You can find other Scripture passages that will dial the focus knob toward more clarity.

Perhaps one of the greatest verses in the Bible states simply, "God is love" (1 John 4:8). Wonderful! But obviously too vague. In what ways is He love? What does that look like? What does it mean? Pick out a Scripture passage that describes God's love in more specific detail—or use Psalm 136—and see how you can focus your understanding of God's love in a way that brings you fresh insight. Then hop on dougnewton.com or the Fresh Eyes app to check out how I used Psalm 136 when searching for a sharper answer.

9

A BIG "IF"

Faith as a Mustard Seed
Matthew 17:20

If I pray for someone's healing and
that person isn't healed, is there
something wrong with me?

If you're sitting at the breakfast table with your family and your sister says, "Please pass the milk," what do you do? Do you pour some milk into the palm of your hand and pour it on her cereal? Of course not. You know what she meant. "Please pass the *milk container*."

Verbal shorthand like that, in this case called *metonymy*, fills our daily language. We encounter a special kind of shorthand, a metonymy, when a news reporter asks a spokesperson for the president, "Does the White House have any comment?" In this case, the White House stands for the official position of the president and his team of advisers. Or when Shakespeare's Mark Antony famously appeals "Friends, Romans, countrymen, lend me your ears" (i.e., "your undivided attention").[1]

Most people develop the ability to recognize such speech nuances by the time they're preteens. Until then, the misunderstandings can be comical. One Christmas season my friend's brilliant six-year-old son saw a poster on a storefront window that stated, JESUS IS THE REASON FOR THE SEASON. The precocious boy shook his head, went up to the lady at the cash register, and complained, "I know Jesus is the reason for Christmas, but the reason for the season is the 23.5-degree tilt of the earth as it revolves around the sun."

A well-known children's book series featuring Amelia Bedelia capitalizes on the humor of taking words too literally. When Amelia is told to "pitch a tent," she literally throws it into the bushes.[2] When told to "weed the garden," she takes that to mean she should plant weeds in the garden.[3] Even small kids understand and giggle over her silly misunderstandings.

However, that doesn't mean it's always easy to tell when something is to be taken literally. We frequently run into this problem in Scripture. Did Jesus mean that you should literally pluck out your eye if it causes you to sin (Mark 9:47)? I knew a person whose brother did just that! Does God have hands and arms and a face? Many Bible verses describe Him that way. Are we supposed to track how many times we forgive someone (Matt. 18:21–22)? If so, it's important to know which translations are correct, because there's a difference of 413 times between forgiving "seventy times seven" and "seventy-seven times." If the statement is literal, we should all hope for the lower number.

Those examples, however, are not too difficult to discern as nonliteral. Don't go plucking out your eyes; just be very aware of how you use them. Don't start counting the number of times you forgive; just keep forgiving. And don't expect God to reach out to touch you with an actual hand or to have an iconic face like Charlton Heston.

However, sometimes we can't tell for sure whether the verse is intended to be understood literally. Sincere Christians come down on different sides of the issue when reading the same verses. For example, when Jesus said we should "turn … the other cheek" (Matt. 5:39), was He meaning we should allow ourselves to be hit a second time? Was He speaking literally when He said to lend money to our enemies and not expect to get anything back (Luke 6:35)? Is the creation account in Genesis referring to six twenty-four-hour days? We have to make up our own minds, prayerfully, on these kinds of statements. That brings me to my experience trying to understand how to take this chapter's famous saying about mountain-moving faith.

DESPERATE DEPENDENCE

A few years ago, I reached a point where I had to know what to make of Jesus' words about moving mountains. I assumed Jesus wasn't encouraging us to go around rearranging the geologic furniture on earth. But clearly, He was calling His disciples, then and now, to break through impossible situations with potent faith. What's more, Jesus embedded this fact of faith in a context of rebuke that meant, *You should have been able to save the boy. If small faith is all it takes to move a mountain, you should have been able to get rid of a measly demon.*

That's where my concern began—in a place of guilt over the lack of mountain-moving results up to that point in my life. I had prayed on numerous occasions for people needing healing who weren't healed. I had also experienced lots of other impossible situations I couldn't budge. So I had to know what I should expect of myself. Was something wrong with me? All I could hear was Jesus saying, "If you had faith … If you had even a little faith …" I could only assume my lack of mountain-moving faith must have been my fault. So I had to know how to understand this frustrating famous saying.

By that point, I had searched the text, the original language, and all the commentaries I had in my library for help. However, more study did not cast a brighter light. I realized that my only hope for insight on this text was a gift of revelation from the Lord.

Before I move on to tell you what I discovered, I am eager to emphasize one wonderful point that puts in proper order everything else this book attempts to teach about having fresh eyes: ultimately, no matter how much we creatively engage with Scripture, we always depend on God's grace to help us see truth.

This moment in my life was simply a case in point. My only hope was to come before the Lord on my knees with this text open and this simple request: "Lord, tell me how to understand this saying." So—talk about being literal—that's exactly what I did. I opened my Bible to this text, laid it on the couch, got on my knees, and told the Lord, "I will not move off this text, I will not study anything else—however long it takes—until You help me see what I need to understand about faith and moving mountains."

THE KEYWORD

The next morning in my devotional time I was back at that spot. And the next. And the next. My Bible open. Praying the same prayer. Reading the same text and nothing else. I did that for at least two weeks, until one morning the simplest thought entered my mind like a key being inserted into a lock. What I saw and confirmed elsewhere in Scripture has become a foundational idea God has used over the years to bring not only freedom from the guilt this verse had previously triggered but also greater boldness to face impossible situations with faith.

The Lord took me to the little word *if* that leads off the conditional clause, "If you have faith." Then He seemed to pose a question: "Who is ultimately responsible for your having faith?"

"Me." I didn't say it out loud, but it seemed like I was in conversation and the Lord asked next, "Really? Children grow if they have food, but is it up to them?"

That question was all it took to launch me into a new way of thinking. Yes, in the Christian life, faith is required. Clearly, Jesus expected the disciples to have faith in this situation. But that does not mean faith is generated by a person's will. None of us can grit our teeth and produce faith by the sweat of our brows. Here's how it comes: faith is a gift of God that is produced by the Word of God in people ready to affirm the truth of God. Let's pull this sentence apart into three sections.

A Gift of God

The fact that faith is a gift from God sometimes gets buried in another famous verse and thus limited in scope. Paul wrote, "For it is by grace you have been saved, through faith—and this is not from yourselves, it is the gift of God—not by works, so that no one can boast" (Eph. 2:8–9).

When Paul wrote "It is the gift of God," the pronoun *it* refers to the whole scenario: being saved by grace through faith. The gift of God is not just salvation and not just grace and not just faith. All of it is a gift, including faith. If not for God's grace we would have neither the capacity for faith nor the content of faith.

Paul's Damascus Road experience certainly formed his viewpoint. The intense light that blinded him physically paradoxically opened his eyes spiritually. He had nothing to do with the inception of his ability to perceive Jesus as the Christ. That faith was a gift of grace. Because of what Paul learned through that experience, he prayed prayers like the following for his people: "I keep asking that the God of our Lord Jesus Christ, the glorious Father, may *give you the Spirit of wisdom and revelation*, so that you may know him better. I pray that *the eyes of your heart may be enlightened* in order *that you may know* the hope to which he has called you" (1:17–18).

It is true—when God opens our minds (the capacity to understand) and dispenses revelation (the content we should understand), He expects us to act on what we come to know. That action is the expression of faith. That is our part. The failure to act in faith is what Jesus rebuked the disciples about. They had the capacity necessary to express faith in that moment, because they had been with Jesus long enough to know what was possible. But for some reason they did not act with the necessary confidence. They had the gift but didn't open it. That was their problem.

Produced by the Word of God

Even though the disciples and people like Paul had the benefit of direct contact with Jesus, that is not necessary for faith to be produced. Paul wrote, "So faith comes from hearing, and hearing through the word of Christ" (Rom. 10:17 ESV). What initiates faith is the spoken Word of God. In fact, according to the apostle John, from the time of creation and beyond, everything God chooses to produce is accomplished through His Word (John 1:3), including faith. So today, when people like you and me engage with the text of Scripture, faith will be produced in us because we are encountering God's words, first spoken by the Spirit, then inscribed on paper. When the disciples and others were in direct physical contact with Jesus, they were engaging with the Word of God made flesh. But whether it's the Word made flesh or God's words made print, it's the Word of God that creates faith.

However, that doesn't occur automatically. If that was the case, then even skeptics and atheists who read Scripture would always wind up as believers.

People Ready to Affirm the Truth of God

The Word of God creates faith in people who are open to the truth of God. Notice that Jesus prefaced His comments about faith that moves mountains with the phrase, "Truly I tell you" (Matt. 17:20). That phrase—or "Verily I say unto you" (KJV) or "Truly I say to you" (NASB)—is an elaborated translation of the words *Amen, amen.*

You probably know that Jesus often prefaced His primary teachings this way. But while it was common for Jesus, it was uncommon in His time. The usual practice then was to conclude prayers or statements of spiritual truth with "Amen." That custom is still practiced today when preachers sometimes conclude their prayers with "And all God's people said …" then wait for the congregation to say "Amen." That custom captures the purpose of the "Amen." It is the way people take the opportunity to say, "So be it. We agree with that. We believe that. That's the way we want it."

So why might Jesus have *begun* His words with "Amen"? By starting with that word, He was emphasizing the importance of affirming whatever He says before we even hear the words. It's as if Jesus was saying, "I'm about to tell you something important, but before I even say it, I expect you to be ready to believe and act on it simply because I am speaking My Father's words."

That readiness to trust whatever God says is the prerequisite for faith being created by the Word of God. You shouldn't wait for more proof. Faith is not likely to be created in those who come to God's Word in stubbornness or skepticism.

GOT UNCTION?

Let's go back to the mountain-moving faith saying so I can show you how liberating this understanding of faith can be. Remember our summary statement: faith is a gift of God that is produced by the Word of God in people ready to affirm the truth of God. If faith comes from God, then whether or not you have faith is not up to you. Your part is to engage consistently with God's Word as someone who already has affirmed it in your heart. Your whole life is to be one big "Amen" to anything God says. If that's your spiritual habit, then from situation to situation God will give you the faith you need to perform anything that is His will. If the faith is not there, that's not necessarily a sign of failure. Rather, it likely points to something that is not God's will at that moment.

Let's take the question of healing as a case in point. Very often sincere Christians get confused about praying for healing. Many times we pray but nothing happens. Did we not have enough faith? Well-meaning fellow Christians might say that is true, using this mountain-moving passage as evidence. "O me of little faith," we moan.

But I have learned how anyone can be freed from that sense of condemnation. *If* you are sincerely and consistently engaging with God through His Word and Spirit and *if* you are cultivating a spirit ready to trust everything God affirms and promises, then He will provide you with a spiritual gift of faith for someone's healing *if* that is His will in that moment.

That gift of faith usually comes with a surge of boldness to pray with unaffected authority—what the old-timers used to call "unction." I have experienced that unction on numerous occasions, like the time I prayed long-distance for a teenager in a distant city who struggled with severe psychological issues that caused bizarre and violent behavior. I had never met him but knew of his parents' desperation for him. One Sunday morning, I gathered my whole congregation of six hundred around the altar to pray for him. I had been fasting for a few days prior, and as I began to pray, a surge of faith overcame me and seemed to flow out of me like lava from a volcano. It was neither my personality nor my practice to speak so boldly in prayer. But that was how the words came out for his complete freedom and healing. Three days later I got word from his father of a remarkable and lasting change in his life that returned him to normalcy.

But *if* that sense of bold faith—that unction—is not present, then you can relax and just offer or, as Scripture says, "present" your requests and petitions with thanksgiving (Phil. 4:6). Then *if* your request is not granted, you do not need to feel guilty as if the lack of faith was your fault. The little "ifs" are your part. But the big "if"—the gift of faith—is up to God.

20/20 FOCUS

1. This chapter claims that Jesus rebuked the disciples' lack of faith as a failure to act on their God-given ability to believe through evidence they had already received. But we should not feel condemned if we lack faith we have not yet been given. Is this a biblically sound distinction? If so, does this help ease your mind?

2. Based on the argument presented in this chapter, put into your own words how you know when to pray boldly for healing versus when to ask humbly.

3. Is there another verse like this mountain-moving verse that confuses you? What is it? How about doing what this chapter describes and bring it before the Lord in prayer until He graciously provides soul-settling insight?

Lord, it is such good news that I can count on You to give me faith when I need it for obedience and bold action. I get so worried—Is there something wrong with me?—when I pray for healing for people but have doubts. Did I just ruin their chance for healing? Now I see the process. I will stay close to You, I will be a person eager to affirm Your words and promises, and I will trust You to give me faith when it's Your will to heal. In the meantime, thank You for the peace that comes when I present my requests. You are good. Amen.

VISION CHECK

All spiritual insight comes as a gift of revelation from God, usually in combination with our searching the Scriptures. Sometimes, however, our only hope for fresh eyes is based not on our effort to study the Word of God but on our waiting for a word from God.

Here's another passage people struggle to understand, so they wind up watering it down or skipping over it. "It is *impossible* for those who have once been enlightened, who have tasted the heavenly gift, who have shared in the Holy Spirit, who have tasted the goodness of the word of God and the powers of the coming age and who have fallen away, to be brought back to repentance. To their loss they are crucifying the Son of God all over again and subjecting him to public disgrace" (Heb. 6:4–6). What does *impossible* mean? Doesn't the Bible say that "with God all things are possible" (Matt. 19:26)? How can it be impossible? When does the "impossible" kick in? Take this question to the Lord over the span of a few days and see what comes to mind. Then compare your insights with mine on dougnewton.com or the Fresh Eyes app.

GOOD NEWS FOR EUNUCHS

House of Prayer or Den of Robbers?
Matthew 21:13

Even if 100 percent of your congregation
comes to daily prayer meetings, that
doesn't mean your church will be a "house
of prayer." Interestingly, what makes a
true house of prayer is not prayer.

I've been hit in the face three times in my life. Once when I was in junior high and riding the school bus, a high school girl did not appreciate how mouthy I was, so she tried to shut my mouth with her fist. The second time came at the hands of my fourth-grade gym teacher. This deserves a more-detailed explanation, as it was a clear case of religious persecution.

I grew up in a family of conscientious objectors, though not to war. My dad was a World War II tank commander in the Battle of the Bulge. Our objection was to something worse than war: dancing. Like many other churches of the day, ours took a stand against drinking, smoking, and dancing. And as a young boy it seemed to me that people involved in such activities were not just bound for hell; they were already citizens there. So when my elementary school's physical education program included the annual do-si-do into square dancing, I neither bowed to my partner nor to school authorities. My refusal was not belligerent, however. All it took was a note from home expressing our church's and family's moral stance against dancing along with a request to be excused. Every year that worked, and I was allowed to skip the week of square dancing, which usually came in the spring.

However, in my fourth-grade year, without warning, the gym teacher substituted a week of square dancing in the fall for the normal week of dodgeball. So when I came to gym class that October day, the record player was already blasting out the twangy sounds of square-dance music. I was horrified. Caught off guard, I had no note from home. What could I do? Without proof of my diplomatic immunity, I would be forced into dance damnation.

Then I thought, *If I make a joke out of it, God will know I'm not wanting to dance and I won't be subject to His wrath.* So I got paired up in the square with the other kids and began to display the dictionary definition of *cavorting.* I cavorted to the left and cavorted to the right, acting a lot like a marionette being controlled by a drunken puppeteer. Actually, I was having fun being a conscientious cavorter, until out of nowhere I was struck to the floor by a blow to the side of my head. The angry gym teacher bellowed, "Newton, quit goofing around!" That's what I think he said. It was hard to make out his words with the ringing in my ears.

These days a gym teacher would be hung by his thumbs for such an act of child abuse. But in my childhood days, persecution produced a compliant fourth grader who immediately moved in every direction the stereophonic caller told me to go.

To be fair to the man, his attack might not have been a case of religious persecution. He could have been having a bad day, or perhaps he felt judged by the unintended moral superiority of all those notes from home he had received over the years, or perhaps it was as simple as his having been a teacher for twenty years. It was probably a combination of those factors.

However, those two memorable blows to my face—along with a bushel of angry rebukes from my parents who might have wanted to smack me themselves for any number of reasons— taught me a lesson: when people get angry, pay attention. They're telling you something about what they think is very important.

TEMPLE TANTRUM

With that in mind, the goal of this chapter is to focus on one moment when Jesus was "fit to be tied" and, by using the study technique of cross-referencing, answer the question, "What was Jesus so passionate about that would make Him so angry?" I'm referring to the time when Jesus stormed through the temple's public area and drove out people who were engaged in the opportunistic "religious" business of money changing and sell- ing small animals for sacrifice. This episode is often referred to as Jesus "cleansing" the temple.

Make no mistake. This was a violent act. Imagine yourself sitting in church during a service when a man bursts into the sanctuary, yelling at the top of his lungs, knocking over pews, pulling down banners, and scattering bulletins. Even if Jesus never struck anyone during His whip-snapping expulsion explosion, people would still have been traumatized as He let His passion loose.

His tirade involved few words. But the two carefully chosen quotations from the Old Testament reveal the reason for His anger, which was not only about the inappropriate business being carried out in the temple but also about the appropriate "business" that was absent: prayer.

John's gospel records what may have been a previous temple cleansing—scholars can't agree—during which Jesus attacked the improper activity: "Stop turning my Father's house into a market!" (John 2:16). His anger that time was turned toward what we might call sins of *commission* (i.e., things happening that shouldn't have been). But in Matthew's account of what is arguably a second event, Jesus' wrath arose over a sin of *omission* (i.e., something that should have been going on but wasn't). That difference gives us good reason to see Jesus' anger with more clarity and gravity.

So let's turn to the Old Testament passages Jesus quoted at the top of His lungs. You will discover how the combination of those Scripture texts helps us see the idea of a house of prayer in an encouraging new light. And surprisingly, a house of prayer is not just about people praying. The two key phrases in Jesus' words are from Isaiah 56:7 ("My house will be called a house of prayer") and Jeremiah 7:11 ("a den of robbers"). Let's take the second one first.

The phrase "den of robbers" is found in a passage where God through Jeremiah accused His people of mistakenly assuming that His temple was automatically a safety zone—that just being there protected them from harm, whether from their enemies or from God's wrath. Jeremiah said, "Do not trust in deceptive words and say, 'This is the temple of the LORD, the temple of the LORD, the temple of the LORD!'" (v. 4).

But the Lord warned His people that their assumption of safety was off the mark if they were engaging in activities that were contrary to His moral laws. They were asked, "Will you steal and murder, commit adultery and perjury, burn incense to Baal and follow other gods you have not known, and then come and stand before me in this house, which bears my Name, and say, 'We are safe'—safe to do all these detestable things?" (vv. 9–10).

In the next verse the Lord used the phrase "den of robbers" because that's where lawbreakers flee, thinking they will escape detection—to their den. "Has this house, which bears my Name, become a den of robbers to you? But I have been watching!" (v. 11).

However, the phrase "den of robbers" doesn't capture the words' true connotation. For these people were more than common thieves; they were government insurgents. They were rebels, working against the purposes of their kingdom. The first-century Jewish scholar Josephus gave the more accurate sense when he compared them to those engaged in "anti-government guerilla warfare."[1]

If that is likely how Jesus used "den of robbers," then He was accusing the people of engaging in activity in the temple that not only neglected kingdom work but even contradicted it. Those were strong words. He was essentially calling them traitors! With that as a backdrop revealing the reason for His violent passion, let's move on to His key reference to Isaiah 56, where we find the phrase "a house of prayer."

A REVERSAL OF POLICY

Isaiah 56 begins with the Lord through the prophet Isaiah forecasting a new era of salvation yet to come: "This is what the LORD says, 'Maintain justice and do what is right, for my salvation is close at hand and my righteousness will soon be revealed'" (v. 1). Although it took a few hundred years for that day to come, Jesus' public ministry ushered in that prophecy's fulfillment. He chose His inaugural words in ministry from another portion of Isaiah proclaiming "the year of the LORD's favor" (Luke 4:18–19) and then periodically announced salvation coming (19:9), the kingdom being at hand (Matt. 3:2; 4:17; 10:7), and righteousness being fulfilled (3:15).

This era of salvation that Isaiah 56 describes involved two categories of people that exemplify a Copernican shift in God's purposes for His temple: foreigners and eunuchs. Formerly people in these categories were explicitly excluded from the Lord's house. The Mosaic law says, "No one who has been emasculated by crushing or cutting may enter the assembly of the LORD. No one born of a forbidden marriage nor any of their descendants may enter the assembly of the LORD, not even in the tenth generation. No Ammonite or Moabite or any of their descendants may enter the assembly of the LORD, not even in the tenth generation" (Deut. 23:1–2).

Down to the tenth generation! However, according to Isaiah, a new day was coming when all of that would be reversed. First, regarding foreigners, the Lord said through Isaiah, "Let no foreigner who is bound to the LORD say, 'The LORD will surely exclude me from his people.' … *These I will bring to my holy mountain* and give them joy in my house of prayer. Their burnt offerings and sacrifices *will be accepted on my altar*" (Isa. 56:3, 7).

Notice that God would give them joy *in* His house of prayer. Those once-excluded foreigners would no longer be excluded. Instead, they would be included—and not just included as visitors with second-class status. The joy of the Lord, which is associated with the blessing of salvation, would be theirs.

The shift that was made possible for the second category of people—eunuchs—was even more remarkable but, following the lead of the passage itself, must be explained delicately. Because of the subject of emasculation—that word itself is conveniently abstract—God's Spirit speaking through Isaiah employed the grace of euphemism: saying gently what can be embarrassingly awkward. (In case you can't guess, the following euphemisms are in italics.) "And let not the eunuch say, 'Behold, I am *a dry tree*.' For thus says the LORD: 'To the eunuchs who keep my Sabbaths, who choose the things that please me and hold fast my covenant, I will give in my house and within my walls *a monument* and a name better than sons and daughters; I will give them an everlasting name *that shall not be cut off*" (vv. 3–5 ESV).

A "dry tree" does not bear fruit or even green leaves. That's euphemism number 1, meaning that eunuchs cannot have children. The word *monument* is the word for "hand," which in the original language was a euphemism for male genitalia. That's euphemism number 2. And finally, using a double entendre, God speaks of an everlasting name that "will not be cut off." That's so graphic it barely qualifies as a euphemism!

Most importantly, notice the promise's power and scope. People who have lost all hope of a significant legacy through offspring will gain eternal significance better than sons and daughters. And where will they receive that blessing? God says, "Within my temple and its walls." We can paraphrase this verse to be promising, "I will give back more than what you lost, resulting in an incredible, irrevocable blessing better than you would have or could have had before."

OPEN ARMS, HEALING HANDS

After revealing this unprecedented change in orientation from exclusion to inclusion, the promising prophecy concludes with the summary statement about the temple that Jesus shouted on that day of cleansing: "For my house will be called a house of prayer for all nations" (Isa. 56:7).

A house of prayer is supposed to be a place where excluded and broken people are welcomed within the embrace of God's inconceivable saving grace and restored to a life better than they ever knew before! In short, true prayer is the expression and action of God's passion to receive and restore broken and outcast people.

Then, to see how God bound Himself to this mission, notice what happened when the gospel spread beyond Jewish Jerusalem to the surrounding non-Jewish world. Who was the first biblical record of a non-Jewish convert from outside Palestine? An Ethiopian eunuch! This wasn't a coincidence. Acts 8:26–29 tells us that God gave Philip, the evangelist, explicit instructions through an angel that led him directly to a eunuch who was reading (coincidentally?) from the prophet Isaiah. God Himself was, as it says of Him in Jeremiah 1:12, "watching to see that [His] word is fulfilled." So once again, we say, a house of prayer is to be a place where

- excluded and broken people are welcomed within the embrace of God's saving grace,

- saving grace is a matter of full restoration,

- and prayer provides the hope of full restoration for people of all nations.

This is why a true house of prayer is not so much about people simply saying prayers but about a spirit of love and an anointing of power that result in incredible inclusion and restoration of broken people. Instead, in the temple, Jesus found only "business affairs" of religion.

If you need any more evidence, look at what happened in the very next verse *after* Jesus drove out the commercial clutter: "The blind and the lame came to him at the temple, and he healed them" (Matt. 21:14). Incredible! If that doesn't prove the point, I don't know what would. The moment the wrong kind of business was removed, a vacuum was created that became filled by the right kind of business: healing and restoring those who had been ceremonially forbidden to enter. That's a true house of prayer. It has little to do with how many people come to prayer meetings and how long they pray.

Remember how I started the chapter saying I have been smacked in the face three times in my life? When I finally understood why Jesus got so mad and what makes a true house of prayer, that was the third time. And I—and the churches I've pastored—have never been the same.

20/20 FOCUS

1. If a true house of prayer is a place where prayer is happening that results in restoring broken people to a condition better than what they've known before, how does your church measure up in that regard?

2. *Inclusion* is a word that is fraught with divisive political overtones these days. For now set politics aside and answer this question: Never mind the arguments over "who" we're talking about, how does the spirit of inclusion behave, based on the Isaiah passage?

3. Think of the symbolism of *foreigners* and *eunuchs*. Who might they represent in our day? Who might you need to embrace with restoring grace?

4. At first glance Jesus' passion to make His temple be what it ought to be is rather shocking, but it is also cause for great hope. How so?

Lord, I was amazed when I discovered in this chapter how You called for a shift in policy from

exclusion to inclusion, from law to grace, regard-
ing foreigners and eunuchs. Your explosive passion
to make that happen in Your temple is beautiful
to behold while at the same time somewhat fright-
ening. I confess I still need to make that shift in
certain areas and toward certain people. Help me
join You in passionately welcoming broken people
into the presence of Your restoring grace, especially
in the way I pray. Amen.

VISION CHECK

Whenever one portion of Scripture contains a quotation from another portion of Scripture, it is important to study that cross-reference. Doing so usually will shed light that gives you fresh eyes for the passage you're studying. Here's one to try.

In Acts 4, Peter and John were jailed and then hauled in front of the city officials over the commotion caused by their healing the lame man in Acts 3. When the magistrates demanded an explanation, Peter quoted Psalm 118:22 and correlated their crucifixion of Jesus with the builders' rejection of the stone (Acts 4:10–11). Read Psalm 118:22 and then Peter's quotation in Acts 4:11. Notice the slight difference and see what you make of it. Then find out what I made of it by going to dougnewton.com or the Fresh Eyes app.

THE FLANNELGRAPH SOLDIER

The Armor of God

Ephesians 6:11

Sometimes the littlest word can make
the biggest difference not only in our
study but also in our prayers.

Long before digital presentations were invented, teachers used flannel. Presenters—often called "Mom" if you grew up in a small country church as I did where all the parents had to take turns teaching Sunday school—did not use a laptop or clicker to advance a slide. They told a story while gradually building an illustration on a four-foot by three-foot, flannel-covered board and placing flannel people and objects one by one on the board. The board was tilted back slightly so the objects would cling—usually—to the flannel background. There was no guarantee Jesus wouldn't droop off the cross before we got to the part where He gave up His spirit. (We tried not to laugh, but you can guess how that went in a class of fourth-grade boys.)

Though that presentation "technology" seems ancient by today's standards, the lessons we learned stuck in our heads. Especially the lesson from this famous portion of Ephesians 6 about the Roman soldier dressing for battle. It probably would have lodged in my ten-year-old head had I seen it only one time. After all, it was about a soldier! But I must have seen that soldier get outfitted for battle well over a hundred times, because we breastplated him and shod his feet and girded his loins (whatever that meant) on a weekly basis during our opening ritual for Christian Youth Crusaders, my boyhood church's sanctified version of Boy Scouts. Ephesians 6:10–17 was the organization's theme text, and it started with "Put on the full armor of God" (v. 11), so that's what we did.

The teacher started by placing a Roman soldier clad in a modest white toga on the flannelgraph. We couldn't have held it together had he started out in "tighty-whities." Then we began to dress him for battle (like a macho Barbie doll).

The teacher asked who wanted to put on the "belt of truth" (v. 14). Hands shot up. I rarely got called on first, since my mom was usually the teacher and could never show favoritism. She handed the flannel belt to someone else, and he walked to the board and laid the belt across the soldier's body, being careful not to knock the soldier off.

"And now we need the breastplate of righteousness ..." Again the hands. Again not me.

His feet got shod with the gospel, which looked more like sandals, and then came the "shield of faith" (v. 16). The "flaming arrows of the evil one" were next (v. 16), but then came my favorite part—the "helmet of salvation" (v. 17). What is it about boys and helmets? Maybe it was also my favorite because it meant we were nearing the end of the exercise, so maybe Mom would call on me. But the last part—and we all knew it—was the "sword of the Spirit" (v. 17), and we all joined the teacher, sounding a bit like pirates proclaiming, "Which is the word of God. A-a-a-a-r-r-r!"

In retrospect, I can't imagine the flannel soldier looked anything but ridiculous. But to us he was ready for battle. We were ready for battle. Against what? We didn't really know, but we were ready for some manly war.

Unfortunately, not only did the image of the flannelgraph soldier stick in our minds, but so did a total misunderstanding of the passage.

THE "AND" IS NEAR

One day while reading this famous passage, I used one of my favorite Fresh Eyes techniques and ignored the reference markers. I started with verse 10 and read it like a letter. It wasn't until then I noticed that verse 17 is not the appropriate end of Paul's thought, even though it was always where we stopped after dressing the flannel soldier: "The sword of the Spirit, which is the word of God." The end. Or so we thought.

Verse 18 begins with *and*. Why was that *and* there? Why had it been disconnected? Grammatically, *and* performs various functions. The two most common purposes are building a list and creating a sequence. You might say, "When I packed the car for vacation, I filled the trunk with suitcases, some food, a couple of books, *and* …" The items you mentioned require no particular order. It's just a list.

However, sometimes the sequence is important. If you need more milk, you'll have to get the keys, open the garage door, back out the driveway, *and* go toward the store. One action follows another *necessarily*.

With that in mind, I went back to the soldier's gear and tried out both options: Is this just a list of various elements identified in no particular order, or is this a sequence of actions? I concluded the best interpretation is to see these verses as a sequence of actions. Even though we weren't Bible scholars, the way we kids dressed the flannelgraph soldier—one step after another—was good Bible interpretation.

So what difference does it make that the *and* indicates a sequence rather than a list? It makes all the difference in the world, because it ties the actions of the soldier's preparation for battle (Eph. 6:14–17) with the actions contained in the next three verses (vv. 18–20): "And *pray in the Spirit* on all occasions with *all kinds of prayers* and requests. With this in mind, be alert and *always keep on praying* for all the Lord's people. *Pray also* for me, that whenever I speak, words may be given me so that I will fearlessly make known the mystery of the gospel, for which I am an ambassador in chains. *Pray* that I may declare it fearlessly, as I should."

These verses begin with the word *and* that links to the sequential actions in the preceding verses. Notice that these three verses emphasize only one activity five times: prayer. When I stumbled upon that observation, my understanding of spiritual warfare instantly did an about-face. The purpose of putting on the armor is to go into *prayer*.

THE BEST DEFENSE IS A GOOD OFFENSE

Since people normally "get dressed" before heading out of the house in the morning, we assume that putting on the armor of God is important preparation for entering the world each day. While it may be, that is not actually what Paul was saying here. Instead, precisely because our battle is *not* against "flesh and blood" (v. 12), we need to put on the whole armor of God—*not* to go into the physical realm of problems but to go into the spiritual realm of prayer. Whatever battles we face must be fought in prayer. We serve the kingdom best in the context of prayer. We withstand the opposition not just by putting on spiritual gear but by putting on spiritual gear and *praying*. That was the reason Paul talked about the armor of God in the first place.

In addition, by missing the significance of the *and* that begins verse 18, we not only locate spiritual warfare incorrectly (*outside* the realm of prayer) but we also have the battle strategy backward. We tend to think of the armor primarily as spiritual protection for heading out into the dangerous world. I have often heard preachers point out that the sword of the Spirit is the only *offensive* element of the soldier's gear. The rest—breastplate, belt, shoes, shield, and helmet—are *defensive*. That's true and not true. It's true the helmet, belt, breastplate, and shield are defensive armor. But that does not mean the soldier is necessarily in a defensive mode. A soldier also wears protective gear when waging an offensive strike.

Because we have failed to link verse 18 to the preceding verses, we picture an enemy advancing against us, requiring us to take defensive measures. It's intended to be the other way around. We are the ones on the offensive. "And pray" (v. 18) was Paul saying "Charge!" The Enemy will try to prevent our attack with a spray of arrows—accusation, skepticism, fear, distraction—and anything else he can throw at us. That's why we need the defensive gear; that's why we must keep standing and not shrink back. But it's not because he is coming against us. Rather, it's because we—the church in prayer—are going against him.

Didn't Jesus say that would be the church's mission and impact? He declared, "I will build my church [offensive tactic]; and the gates of hell shall not prevail against it" (Matt. 16:18 KJV). We are ramming the ramparts of enemy strongholds when we engage in prayer.

There's a good picture of this scenario in Mark 4:35–41. In one of my other books in this series, *Fresh Eyes on Jesus' Miracles*,

I pointed out how the life-threatening storm at sea that battered Jesus and the disciples was a demonic attempt to resist the kingdom's advance into new territory where an enemy stronghold existed. Rather than turning back in fear, Jesus showed the disciples how to remain firm and keep advancing. This is what Paul was talking about here in Ephesians 6.

This perspective shift that comes from understanding the role of the word *and* makes a huge difference in how we live and shapes our expectations about the church's impact on the world around us. *And* it points us toward the most important kingdom work—prayer.

TWO WORTHWHILE TATTOOS

Church history supports this perspective. Scores of books over the centuries have documented prayer as the single most important catalyst of revival movements and the expansion of God's kingdom around the world. Indeed, at this point we could spend multiple chapters exploring prayer and how it functions as a transformational instrument. But that topic is too big for now and takes us away from two action points that are much more focused and personal.

First, don't do anything to solve a problem until you've prayed. If we move in the flow of Paul's Spirit-inspired admonition, then no matter what problems we encounter, we should never face them as problems of a purely human ("flesh and blood") nature. That does not mean we should treat every problem as something demons caused. It simply means that our first priority—before we do anything else—is to put on the armor of God and enter a season of prayer during which we arrest any possible shenanigans of our spiritual Enemy.

In that sense, prayer is like what emergency room doctors and nurses do. Their job often is to stabilize victims so the ultimate treatment needed to bring recovery can occur safely and effectively. Prayer is what we do to thwart the Enemy's obstructive and destructive efforts so that the power of God's Spirit and wisdom can work effectively through people or circumstances to bring solutions. This is such an important point that it might be helpful to tattoo your forearm as a reminder: *I will do nothing to address any problem until I've prayed.* Seriously.

Second, let the Word and Spirit form your prayers. The text suggests the armor is to protect the soldier on the attack. And if the sword is the only offensive weapon *mentioned*, then the Word of God is the only offensive weapon *needed*! Since God ordained this, you can count on the revealing and empowering help of God's Spirit when you intentionally employ words of Scripture in the development of your prayers. As you search the Scriptures to find promises and truths that fit the problem you're praying about, God's Spirit shapes and sharpens those words into prayers that cut through the Enemy's schemes.

Over the years I have known many people who have been assailed by tormenting thoughts of all kinds—to the point they were afraid of engaging in normal activities like sleep, conversation, human contact, eating certain foods, or making ordinary decisions. Most of these folks overcame those fears by employing scriptural truth in their prayers. Jesus Himself modeled this technique when He faced down the Devil during His famous three temptations (Luke 4:1–13).

One day a young mom approached a small group of fellow believers after our church service. She'd endured a debilitating case of crushing self-condemnation and the inability to grasp God's love for her. As we prayed, several people relied on Scripture to declare her worth in God's sight, and they couched their encouragement in Spirit-prompted images for her to hold on to. Still, she struggled to believe these affirmations. That's when one group member thought of some Scriptures that speak of the importance of childlike faith and converted that concept into a bold request: "Lord, Becky is having a hard time believing that she has great worth in Your sight, so I ask You to use her three-year-old daughter to affirm that message in some way that helps her to know it's true."

The prayer time ended, and Becky left to pick up her two kids from the church nursery. As she loaded her one-year-old into a car seat, her daughter—remember she's just three—sat down on the curb, waiting to get in the car. Becky turned to look at her, and the little girl had her head bowed. "What are you doing, sweetheart?"

"I'm praying for you, Mama." Becky's daughter had never done this before and had no idea of her mother's struggle. Becky immediately recognized it as an answer to prayer and later reported how at key moments in the following weeks her daughter again said or prayed something encouraging out of the blue. This happened too many times for Becky not to see it as God's miraculous answer to a specific prayer based on the use of God's Word.

So … "put on the full armor of God" (Eph. 6:11)? Yes, and fight the winning battle in prayer. Years ago when my mom and other faithful parents entered their rotation in the annual Who's Gonna Take the Fourth Graders This Year? draft, I bet none of them imagined how long the lesson of a flannelgraph soldier would stick in a young boy's mind. But it did. I since have learned that these and many other adults were not just teaching but were also faithfully praying for us kids all those years. Clearly, these godly people were very good with a sword!

20/20 FOCUS

1. People with "activist" tendencies struggle with prayer, because it doesn't feel as if you're getting

anything done. If you're like that, does Paul's aggressive image of prayer help you get over that hump?

2. Even though the Bible never uses the term *spiritual warfare*, plenty of Scriptures use battle imagery and terminology in reference to spiritual matters. See how many you can come up with in just a few minutes. Here's one example to get you started: "We are more than *conquerors*" (Rom. 8:37).

3. If prayer is designed, in part, to bring God's power against all forms of spiritual opposition, think of a situation (personal, local, or national) you could pray about more aggressively.

4. Work your way through each element of the soldier's gear and consider how those elements might function in the context of prayer.

Lord, it's fitting that the last chapter and prayer in this book are about prayer. As I read this passage now with fresh eyes, my heart responds with new excitement about the privilege and power of prayer. Please write this lesson indelibly on my

heart so I never forget and drift away from prayer
as my primary way of advancing Your kingdom.
Amen.

VISION CHECK

Conjunctions (like *and, but, nor,* and *or*) and conjunctive adverbs (like *therefore, consequently, however,* and *moreover*) are important connectors between ideas, but they often get overlooked. However, whenever you come across one, you should discover its purpose. As they say, what is *therefore* there for? Treat conjunctions like speed bumps that slow down your thinking.

Read the famous story about Jesus visiting Mary and Martha's home (Luke 10:38–42). There you will find the word *but* used twice. Since that word always indicates things in contrast, spend extra time thinking more deeply about what is being contrasted in each case. You will probably see something new that likely has not been the passage's focus when you've heard it taught. See what I discovered by going to dougnewton.com or the Fresh Eyes app.

NOTES

CHAPTER 2

1. Maria MacLachlan, "The Golden Rule," Think Humanism, October 2007, www.thinkhumanism.com/the-golden-rule.html.

2. Confucius, *The Analects*, trans. David Hinton (Washington, DC: Counterpoint, 1998), 176.

3. Udānavarga 5:18, *Udanavarga: A Collection of Verses from the Buddhist Canon*, ed. W. Woodville Rockhill, comp. Dharmatrâta (London: Trübner, 1883), 27.

4. "The Law of Love," MegaInsights, accessed February 19, 2018, www.megainsights.com/the-law-of-love/.

5. *The Mahabharata*, Book 12: *Santi Parva* 167, accessed March 9, 2018, www.sacred-texts.com/hin/m12/m12a166.htm.

6. Hans Küng and Walter Homolka, *How to Do Good and Avoid Evil: A Global Ethic from the Sources of Judaism*, trans. John Bowden (Woodstock, VT: SkyLight Paths, 2009), 38.

7. Ed Russo, trans., *You Are Buddha: Translation of the Vajrayana* (Pittsburgh, PA: Illuminated, 2014), 25–26.

8. Dorothy Littell Greco, "Chick-Fil-A's Lesson on Loving Your Enemies," *Christianity Today*, February 2013, www.christianitytoday.com/women /2013/february/chick-fil-as-lesson-on-loving-your-enemies.html.

CHAPTER 5

1. Steven Johnson, *Mind Wide Open: Your Brain and the Neuroscience of Everyday Life* (New York: Scribner, 2004), 30–31.

2. Olga Khazan, "Meaningful Activities Protect the Brain from Depression," *Atlantic*, April 21, 2014, www.theatlantic.com/health/archive/2014/04/how-meaningful-activities-protect-the-teen-brain-from-depression/360988/; Blake A. Allan et al., "Meaningful Work and Mental Health: Job Satisfaction as a Moderator," *Journal of Mental Health* 28, no. 1 (2018): 38–44.

CHAPTER 8

1. Craig Keener, *Miracles: The Credibility of the New Testament Accounts, Volumes 1 and 2* (Grand Rapids, MI: Baker Academic, 2011).

CHAPTER 9

1. William Shakespeare, *The Tragedy of Julius Caesar*, ed. Barbara A. Mowat and Paul Werstine (New York: Simon & Schuster, 2011), 121.

2. Peggy Parish, *Amelia Bedelia Goes Camping* (New York: HarperCollins, 2003), 28–30.

3. Peggy Parish, *Amelia Bedelia Helps Out* (New York: Greenwillow Books, 1979), 11–13.

CHAPTER 10

1. William L. Lane, *The Gospel According to Mark*, The New International Commentary on the New Testament (Grand Rapids, MI: Eerdmans, 1974), 407.

1

GOT WINE?

Turning Water into Wine
John 2:1–11

If God is able to turn water into wine, why
don't we see more cases of transformation
in people and circumstances?

I pastored for years in southern Kentucky, where the humid summers make you sweat like a cold glass of sweet iced tea. This was usually not a problem, provided you could go from your air-conditioned home to your air-conditioned car to your air-conditioned workplace to the air-conditioned store.

But on too many occasions I had the misfortune of performing weddings in non-air-conditioned churches chosen for their quaint ambience. Funny how the allure of ambience wilts as the congregation waits for the bride's entry. Every bride wants a perfect wedding day. Did no one think the lack of air conditioning might be a distracting discomfort? Oh well …

Some things are the same in all places at all times. Weddings need to go well. That's why even two thousand years later we can relate to the first miracle the apostle John recorded in his gospel. It occurred during a wedding in Cana. The problem at this wedding was not drenching humidity but the disappointing lack of celebratory wine.

Before we delve into the miracle and discover something you may never have thought about, it's important to realize that this miracle holds a special place in the New Testament Gospels. Only John's gospel tells it. Matthew, Mark, and Luke for some reason did not include it. On top of that, John handpicked just seven miracles out of scores he could have chosen. He did so because his mission differed from the other gospel writers'. The few miracles he chose ranked at the top of all Jesus' miracles, because in John's mind they were not just supernatural wonders. They were "miraculous signs" pointing to Jesus' divine identity and unique mission.

John chose this miraculous sign to be the first—the leadoff hitter for his whole story of Jesus' glory. We can only guess why. But what could be a better start to the gospel of Jesus than to show Him to be the one who can do miracles of transformation? Isn't that what everyone needs?

John started by saying, "On the third day a wedding took place at Cana in Galilee. Jesus' mother was there, and Jesus and his disciples had also been invited to the wedding. When the wine was gone, Jesus' mother said to him, 'They have no more wine'" (John 2:1–3).

Notice those last five words Jesus' mother spoke. Don't just read them. Imagine them. What did she sound like when she voiced them? Certainly she wasn't flat and emotionless like a computer speech synthesizer: "They … have … no … more … wine."

Imagine her tone of voice. Her volume. Her intensity. A little cultural background might help inform your imagination.

In those days, wedding celebrations were major events that often lasted several days. You think wedding planners today have a chore? Imagine having the job of "master of the banquet." Some translations even call that person the "governor of the feast" (KJV). A wedding celebration was no small affair if it required a governor to be in charge!

With so much riding on a wedding celebration attended by the whole town, you can imagine the potential outcry if things went poorly. In fact, according to historians, running out of wine at a wedding celebration was grounds for a lawsuit! And you thought we live in a litigious society?

That's why worry and a shot of desperation probably resonated in Jesus' mother's voice. Perhaps she pulled Jesus aside and whispered it, but there would have been a lot of force behind those words, like a pressure valve releasing pent-up steam: "They have no more wine!"

If you, like me, grew up in a teetotaler home, running out of wine would cause great relief not grave consternation. So I wonder what would give me a similar level of concern, considering my upbringing. Here's the best I can do: What if they ran out of wedding cake, the kind I love piled high with frosting? I imagine myself attending a wedding in the humid Kentucky heat … and trapped in a church basement after the ceremony, waiting uncomfortably, dress shirt sticking to the back of the chair … longing for—no, praying for—the good fortune of getting a corner piece of cake adorned with a creamy confection rose. Then finally getting to the buffet table and finding they've run out of cake! Yes, I would be considering a lawsuit! Or maybe something even worse involving that cake knife!

Somehow that imagined scenario puts me in a place where I can hear Mary's panic when she cries, "They have no more wine." Yet despite her desperation, Jesus seemed unmoved. Let's read on: "'Woman, why do you involve me?' Jesus replied. 'My hour has not yet come'" (John 2:4).

How would you like to get a Mother's Day card addressed "Woman"? Maybe that was a respectful form of address in Jesus' day, but He still sounds reluctant to help. Is He really being unsympathetic? Probably not. He was making a theological point. When He referred to "my hour," He was not talking about clock time. The word used here refers to a "special moment." He typically referred to His eventual death on the cross this way.

Jesus was putting things in proper perspective. He knew His mother wanted Him to use His supernatural ability to fix the problem, which He knew would reveal something about His amazing identity. But was it time for that? Shouldn't He reserve that revelation for a greater display of glory than solving this wine shortage? I can almost hear Him say, "I came into this world to save much more than one wedding." That's where He was probably coming from when He replied to His mother.

Amusingly, Jesus' mother didn't seem to wait for His reply before she was off rounding up the servants. After all, she was His mother. She knew her boy. She didn't need to wait for an answer before assuming He would help. John recorded, "His mother said to the servants, 'Do whatever he tells you.' Nearby stood six stone water jars, the kind used by the Jews for ceremonial washing, each holding from twenty to thirty gallons" (vv. 5–6).

Remember that fact given about the stone water jars. We'll come back to them.

Jesus ordered the servants to fill the jars with water and then take a sample of the water to the master of the banquet. When they did that, the feast master, not knowing the whole story, enjoyed what he considered a fine glass of wine. But that puzzled him: "Then he called the bridegroom aside and said, 'Everyone brings out the choice wine first and then the cheaper wine after the guests have had too much to drink; but you have saved the best till now'" (vv. 9–10).

Not only did Jesus convert water into wine, but it was not the boxed variety! This wine would impress the snootiest waiter at restaurants where common people can't even afford to pay for parking.

Think about that. Jesus took water, which consists of only two elements: two parts hydrogen, one part oxygen (H_2O). Not only did He remix those two elements, but he also added the element carbon. We know that because the natural sugars in wine grapes include carbon. And He introduced many more compounds that never existed in the water. Wine includes tannins and organic acids: tartaric, malic, and citric. In short, He didn't just sneak some red food coloring into the water when no one was looking. He somehow accelerated the aging process and turned two minutes into years, as far as the wine was concerned.

Without even waving His hand or whispering "Abracadabra," Jesus performed a miracle of radical transformation. Only the God who created the universe from nothing could have infused the one-time water with carbon and acids and sparkling flavor. If He could do this to water-filled pots, imagine what He can do with worry-filled people. Imagine how He can create unexpectedly high-quality wisdom or faith or peace where none exists.

Isn't this the basis of our hope, our only hope—that God performs miracles of transformation? So let's return to the teaser question at the head of this chapter: If God is able to turn water into wine, why don't we see more cases of transformation in people and circumstances?

The answer emerges when we backtrack to the command Jesus gave the servants and note their response. Remember, Jesus told them to fill the waterpots. Picture those waterpots. Recall that each one held twenty to thirty gallons of water, so they were about the size of a standard galvanized trashcan, except made of stone.

How would the servants have fulfilled Jesus' command? Would they have pulled out the garden hose, attached it to a house spigot, and lopped it over the top? Probably not.

Would they have carried the waterpots to the town well, filled them, and lugged them back to the festivities? Thirty gallons of water weighs about 250 pounds, and that's on top of the weight of the stone waterpots themselves. No way would even two people be able to carry such a heavy, sloshing, unwieldy container. Even a donkey cart would have proved pointless no matter how hard you tried to keep the pots steady and level over the rough paths.

So how would they have filled the waterpots? By carrying small buckets back and forth from the well, probably located some distance away, over and over again until the pots were full.

I'm a pretty hard worker, but the idea of hauling water back and forth in little two-gallon animal skin buckets would not have been a pleasant thought. Bear in mind I probably had already filled those waterpots earlier in the day.

What would I have done? What would you have done? We should not zip right past this question in order to get on with the miracle story. I got out my calculator and estimated it would have taken about eighty trips back and forth to obey Jesus' command. Or perhaps only forty trips if using a neck yoke for carrying two skins at a time. Either way, the task was time consuming and labor intensive.

If I had been a servant in this story, I might have filled the first waterpot to within a couple inches of the top, thought *That's good enough*, and started filling waterpot number two. I would have filled that one to within perhaps three or four inches of the top, thought again *That's good enough*, and started in on waterpot number three. I would have filled pot three to within five or six inches…. You see where I'm going? My enthusiasm to fulfill Jesus' command would have been draining out even as I was filling the waterpots, until maybe—maybe—the sixth and final waterpot would have been about half-full when I decided to draw one more bucket and a final conclusion: *That's good enough.*

However, here's the shocking observation about the text. John carefully pointed out that the servants "filled them to the brim" (John 2:7). Most servants in this culture could choose how they went about their work, like employees in our day. That's why in several places the New Testament urges Christian servants to work diligently and with good attitudes as an act of worship and witness. I must confess the servants at the wedding were more thorough and diligent than I would have been. But what difference does it make whether they filled the waterpots to the maximum level?

Here's the difference. Imagine my sixth half-full waterpot containing only fifteen gallons of water compared with the actual servants' completely full waterpot. How much wine would I have gotten? Fifteen gallons. How many gallons of wine would they have gotten? Thirty. If I had brought five gallons of water, how much wine would I have gotten? Five gallons. Do you see the point?

Yes, Jesus could have turned a thimble of water into thirty gallons of wine. But John reported a miracle not of multiplication but of transformation. Jesus intentionally "revealed his glory" (v. 11) by changing the quality not the quantity of the substance brought to Him. He could have snapped His fingers and created enough wine for a thousand weddings, but He chose to remedy the wine shortage by telling the servants to bring to Him what needed to be changed.

Only Jesus could have performed the miracle of transformation. He took H_2O and made an elegant combination of elements, tannin, bouquet, and color—from water to fine wine—without touching, adding, mixing, or blending any additional ingredients. But the amount of water that was transformed depended on how much water the servants brought. Had they brought less water, less would have been transformed.

That's the lesson for us. It turns out that the old gospel song has been right all along:

> What a Friend we have in Jesus,
> All our sins and griefs to bear!
> What a privilege to carry
> Everything to God in prayer!
> O what peace we often forfeit,
> O what needless pain we bear,
> All because we do not carry
> Everything to God in prayer.[1]

Why don't we see more transformation in people and circumstances? The amount of wine we enjoy depends on the amount of water—things that need to be changed—we bring to Jesus, particularly when brought in the waterpots of prayer. How many gallons are you bringing?

Documentation and analyses of spiritual revivals throughout history reveal that prior to these events, people "filled [the waterpots] to the brim" with prayer. What is true of widespread revivals is true of restored marriages, rescued addicts, redeemed prodigals, and rejuvenated hope: prayer should be thorough to the point of nearly overflowing. Whatever needs to be transformed, take it to Jesus in prayer. And do not stop until you experience an incredible transformation either in your world or in how you see it.

It will be like getting the corner piece of a wedding cake over and over again.

20/20 FOCUS

1. In Scripture, miracles often include some human involvement. Can you think of other biblical examples when human involvement contributed to the occurrence or impact of a miracle? What does that reveal about God's purposes? Why do you think He'd want us contributing to His miracles?

2. What more do you need to bring to Jesus to be transformed in prayer?

3. Have you ever truly considered how much forfeited peace and needless pain we suffer from not bringing "everything to God in prayer"? Why do you think you have had a hard time filling the waterpots with prayer?

4. Is there something else you saw in this story that changes the way you understand it?

Lord, I thank You that You alone can utterly transform any resource, any situation, or any person into something brand new, exciting, and more fitting to Your purpose. Forgive my lack of trust and when I withhold things, try to fix my problems, and attempt change myself or my situations without looking to You first. Help me fill my life up with prayer to the brim. Amen.

VISION CHECK

The study technique this chapter employed involves more fully imagining yourself in the story. Ask, *What would I have been experiencing in this situation?*

Read Genesis 12, which tells of God's promise to Abram to make him the father of a great nation. Put yourself in Abram's situation as an elderly man with a barren wife. What might you have been thinking had you been in his place? Write down what insights come to mind and, using dougnewton.com or the Fresh Eyes app, compare them with a few that came to my mind.

NOTE

1. Joseph Scriven, "What a Friend We Have in Jesus," 1855, public domain.

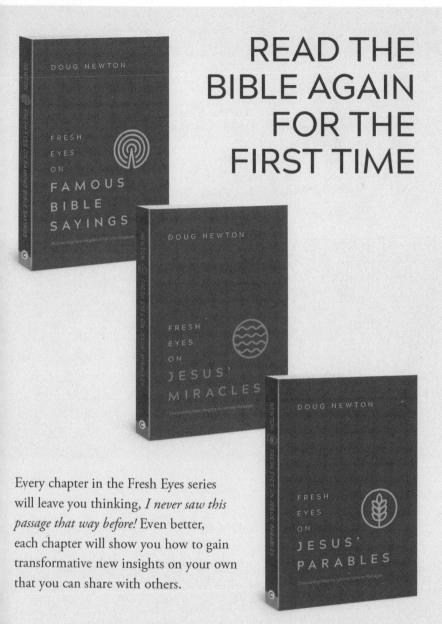

FRESH EYES

VISIT
WWW.DOUGNEWTON.COM

- · Learn more and connect with the author
- · Be the first to learn about new projects
- · Find out if Doug is speaking near you
- · Get brand new, fresh content